P9-DMX-770

WITHDRAWN

WITHDRAWN

THE ECONOMIC
INTERPRETATION OF HISTORY

Also Published in

REPRINTS OF ECONOMIC CLASSICS

By HENRI SEE

MODERN CAPITALISM [1928]

THE ECONOMIC INTERPRETATION OF HISTORY

By

HENRI SÉE

Professor Emeritus, University of Rennes

Translation and Introduction by

MELVIN M. KNIGHT

Reprints of Economic Classics

AUGUSTUS M. KELLEY PUBLISHERS

New York 1968

Translation of French Edition First Published 1929

(New York: Adelphi Company, 1929)

Reprinted 1968 by
AUGUSTUS M. KELLEY   PUBLISHERS
New York   New York   10010

LIBRARY OF CONGRESS CATALOGUE CARD NUMBER

67 - 30863

PRINTED IN THE UNITED STATES OF AMERICA
by SENTRY PRESS, NEW YORK, N. Y. 10019

CONTENTS

PREFACE

The question of the economic interpretation of history has been the author's chief concern in this work. Do economic phenomena furnish the key to all historical evolution? If not absolutely preponderant, what is their real importance? This is the problem of historical knowledge which it is proposed to examine. Since, however, the economic interpretation is so closely bound up with the materialistic conception of history, the first part of the book is devoted to the character and genesis of this doctrine.

The reader need not, therefore, expect to find a detailed history of the Marxian doctrine and its evolution. The aim has been simply to describe the genesis of the materialistic conception of history, to determine its character and to test it in the light of contemporary facts and historical data. Does the doctrine clash with the truth as historical criticism reveals it to us, and if so, to what extent? These are the fundamental questions examined. With entire impartiality, and as objectively as possible, an attempt has been made to estimate the strength and weakness of a doctrine which has not only had its practical effect on the masses but has also exerted an important influence on history, on political and social economy, and on sociology.

This is equivalent to saying that the author has resolutely tried to keep himself aloof from all political and social prejudices, if not completely to rise above them. The account will perhaps offend sincere convictions, and it is possible also that the enemies of socialism will try to find support in certain criticisms which are in no wise directed against the doctrine of socialism as a whole. No account can be taken of these possibilities. It seems best simply to assume that historical and philosophical research is not obliged to take a position on any dogma whatever.

It is precisely because of the assumption of such an attitude that this essay may perhaps have a certain value. Too often studies in the materialistic conception of history take the form of apologies or diatribes. It is true that genuinely scientific treatises have been devoted to it, such as those of L. Woltmann, E. R. A. Seligman, V. G. Simkhovitch, and C. Barbagallo, but whatever the merit of these authors, none of them has undertaken to study the doctrine as a function of the problem of historical knowledge.[1] Nevertheless the author owes much to his predecessors, who have greatly facilitated his own investigations. He has also found a valuable guide in the discriminating book of Edward Bernstein, *Evolutionary Socialism*, which, although the work of a man of action and a militant socialist, is permeated with a remarkably scientific spirit.

---

[1] An exception is Kurt Breysig, in the second volume of his very interesting work: *Vom geschichtlichen Werden* (1925–26), which the author has read with great profit.

THOUGH it may seem like gilding the lily, I shall try to follow Professor Sée's wishes and point out as clearly as possible in an introduction what seem to be the main differences in background and ideas between the American and Continental European readers of a book on this subject. To begin with, some of the Marxian terminology in use in France has never become current in the United States. Even the French title of this book (*Matérialisme historique et interprétation économique de l'histoire*) sounds clumsy in English if literally translated. Back of the economic interpretation lies a philosophy which we awkwardly designate as the "materialistic conception of history," generally called "historical materialism" on the Continent of Europe. This expression is not common in English, though it has been used, for example as the title of a small volume of critical essays by Benedetto Croce, and that of a long communist apology by Bukharin. This slight hitch in translating the title is evidently not the only case of the kind encountered in the book. The background of ideas, experience and social structure common to author and public in

9

France, Germany or Italy is not exactly that suggested by reading American history or observing contemporary life in most parts of the United States. Some expressions, such as *"histoire-science,"* though perfectly definite in French, have no exact equivalents in our language because the division of labor they represent is really somewhat different in this country.

To an American student of Marxism, the materialistic conception and the economic interpretation of history will seem to be merely different aspects of the same thing. It is one peculiarity of our history that our "proletariat," in so far as we have one in the European sense of the term, has on an average arrived from Europe much more recently than is the case with our population in general. The difficulty about terminology hardly exists for those who still have clear memories of European life, or of one of the Continental languages. There is, however, a large group of possible readers to whom the economic interpretation of history may not mean Marxism, or even socialism, the term having been widely used in America by non-socialists. Due to the relatively smaller number affiliated with socialist political parties in the United States than in Europe, the people familiar with the party dogmas as a matter of course are likewise fewer. These dogmas mean very little to innumerable moderate socialists in Europe, but they furnish a framework of ideas which the American liberal does not have, and is therefore free to think of the economic factors in history in much more general terms.

American history has been economic history to a peculiar degree, due at least in part to the fact that other things prominent in Europe have been kept in the background here. We have had only one fundamentally important war since we gained our independence. It was not an international conflict, but a case of secession arising from domestic social and economic differences. Rival political forces were joined, it is true, but it was unusually obvious that these were the shadows of more substantial issues. Only occasionally have diplomatic relations been vital to our national life, and our frontier communities have required less than the usual amount of political machinery.

Our seaboard colonies were established in the great days of the chartered companies, and in part through their agency. The distance from Europe, the strange conditions, and the emphasis upon economic rather than political organization, almost painlessly separated these earliest immigrants and their descendants from many vestiges of medieval social machinery which Europe did not get rid of so easily in the changing times. Old, densely settled countries are always hampered by want of room in carrying out sweeping economic changes. There is a lack of available surplus, not required for the maintenance of existing population, standards of living and the fabric of institutions. Europe still had an ancient and well-knit structure of agriculture, industry and commerce—including world trade—to keep going and feed millions of people, even though much of it was known to be obsolete. America had almost illimitable good land, and was able to draw upon European manufactures. It was not the pioneers single-handed who conquered the wilderness —they were the cutting edge of an old and powerfully organized civilization. The slight political needs of frontier settlements have been amply commented upon; but too little attention has been paid to the social effects of constant migration in checking the growth of family prestige, and hence of the cliques based upon it in more stationary societies.

Samuel Seabury, the loyalist pamphleteer of the American Revolution, was an economic interpretationist nearly a half century before Marx's birth, as was also the then adolescent Alexander Hamilton who answered the broadsides. Both had their eighteenth-century antecedents, some of whom can be accurately traced. As a mature man, Hamilton wrote his famous *Report on Manufactures*, laying down a philosophy of American history to date as well as a program. By 1800, the United States was definitely launched upon a career of westward expansion. The cotton gin had been invented to supply the new textile machinery with fiber—especially in Europe. A new agrarianism was born, of which the frontiers were to be temporary for most of a century. No longer was America an Atlantic fringe, in easy contact with the mother continent of her civilization. Jefferson, a perfectly good eighteenth-century *philosophe* who was as much at home in France as in America, lived to see his country swing very far from the liberal and deistic cosmopolitanism of the American and French Revolutions.

During a long bucolic period we had no real philosophy of history, and most of our population had no sophisticated philosophy of any kind. How much higher education was diluted in the expanding society has been pointed out repeatedly, for example by Dixon Ryan Fox. The small groups on our Atlantic seaboard which kept intellectually in touch with Europe mainly did so at the expense of losing contact with those parts of the United States where life was quite non-European, and where a distinctively American society was in the making. In a country with a rapidly moving frontier and plenty of free or cheap land, no peasantry was formed, at all comparable to that of Europe. For the same reason, among others, the terms "proletariat" and "class struggle" have never conveyed their European significance—emotional as well as descriptive—to the majority of American readers. Karl Marx's attempt to set the Hegelian dialectic "on its feet" instead of "on its head" by giving it a materialistic basis in place of the idealistic one left us cold. America had not been in a philosophical frame of mind during the period when Hegel's system of thought reigned supreme. We had no overcrowded agricultural regions to draw upon for proletarians—in fact many Americans were alarmed at the flow of people in the opposite direction, from Eastern towns to Western farms. Under these circumstances, the new social and political propaganda did not seem to mean much in agrarian America, and the revision of Hegel as a prop provoked relatively slight interest.

Our special conditions have been associated with ideas of their own, some of which have resisted Marxism. From the days of Hamilton, American statesmen have generally recognized the fact that our economic situation is peculiar. There has been some good work on the westward movement all along, but it remained for Frederick Jackson Turner to make this the central theme in presenting American history. His largely economic and geographic interpretation has steadily made its way since 1893, because it gives a realistic picture of the peculiarities of our historical development, and in spite of the fact that it is as far as possible from the Marxian epic of a class struggle. We have had our Marxists, but those among them

who have been both able and extreme have not suc-
ceeded in holding the majority even of our relatively
small socialist group for any length of time.

Of this much it is necessary only to remind the
reader of a book of this kind. Before going into the
American economic interpretations (always in the
plural), it may be well to mention the real excuse for
the length of this introduction. There is one source of
resistance to Marxism in this country and generation
which has attracted no attention, but which undoubtedly goes a long way toward robbing the movement of the mixture of enthusiastic and intellectually
competent leadership so necessary to real vitality.
Most of the intelligent and well informed younger
socialists are aware of a new technique, adapted to prediction in the social sciences, which has developed into
a practical instrument and has been applied to actual
life on a vast scale within the past three or four decades. I refer to statistics, not merely in the older sense
of a quantitative arrangement of data, but also in the
newer one of a mathematical tool capable of discover-
ing and expressing degrees of relationship. Prediction
involves assumptions about the repetition of past ex-
periences or their component factors which can be
verified or measured only by much more exact and complicated methods than those envisaged when the Marxian philosophy was taking shape.

ECONOMIC INTERPRETATION OF HISTORY

Leaving until later the details of the general problem this raises, it may be remarked at this point that the practical application of this technique to the economic phenomena with which this book is chiefly concerned has gone much further in America than, for example, in France. Let there be no vagueness as to the exact meaning intended. European mathematicians and other scientists laid the foundations. What Americans did was to adopt the procedure when it had reached the practical stage, adapt it ingeniously to the problems of actual life, and make its use so general that it touches the interests of everyone and the consciousness of most people. We are now the nation of forecasters *par excellence*. If our enthusiasm has carried us too far, this in no way alters the main point, which is that Americans are generally aware of mathematical systems of prediction, surrounded by an atmosphere of scientific method which makes the old verbal analyses of rhythms of events look like child's play. The public propagandist of any other scheme in the United States must be prepared to answer questions about this one, or run the risk of being made a fool of by some person in his audience with a working or a reading knowledge of current forecasting methods. And one who is prepared to answer serious questions of this kind knows enough to dampen his evangelical enthusiasm for any simpler procedure.

INTRODUCTION TO THE AMERICAN EDITION

French newspapers have carried popular expositions of our methods which read like similar American attempts to explain Einstein to those who do not know algebra. Though the scientific work which made this prediction technique possible was much more French than American, we have played the practical rôle of engineers or inventors—original only in the sense of ingenuity in the application and amplification of others' ideas. What I am dealing with here is the "popular mind," for it is the reception of social propaganda there which counts. Yet a distinction exists even in the case of specially educated classes. I have before me a photostatic copy of a course of instruction given at the University of Paris in 1927–28 on present-day economic statistics. One of the three parts is devoted to forecasting. The sources given are almost entirely American. All this has injected caution into economic interpretations of history, especially in the United States. There is even a tendency for historians to stick to the past and the present, leaving the forecasts to those who have special training, and some experience with the limitations involved.

This is no place for a catalogue of even the greatest names associated with what has often been a frankly economic view of American history. The writings of Charles A. Beard are perhaps the most familiar example because they are the most widely read. He has a habit of illustrating the tendency of people in private life to pursue what they consider to be their interests, and of public men generally to attempt to follow the interests of their constituents. Mistakes in judgment occur in both cases, sometimes leading even to wars, and it is not always possible for the statesman to separate the two types of interests in his single mind. With Beard, economic phenomena are given the central position in a broadly eclectic interpretation because they are the most convenient to handle—to identify in the movements through time and space with which the writer of history must deal. Far from embracing the rigid determinism of the Marxians, Beard has loved in his class lectures to quote from Bossuet that "men do other than they intend," and "it is not ours to force the iron gates of the future." One may read Hegel, and use his thought or terminology as an historical tool, without being a disciple of Marx. In fact, as Veblen remarked long ago, Marx's economic materialism was never able entirely to make its peace with the newer ideas about the material world which came in with Darwin and Wallace.

Arthur W. Calhoun, who of our competent scholars perhaps comes nearest to orthodox economic determinism, chided people like Bober (in the course of a review of the latter's book, *Karl Marx's Interpretation of History* in the American Economic Review for

June, 1928) for passing "a twentieth century judgment on a nineteenth century hypothesis without first taking pains to see what the hypothesis would look like if rewritten in current terms." Calhoun proceeded to characterize the economic interpretation of history as "but a sociological extension of the theory of biologic evolution." Incidentally, this is not what the social doctrine meant to Marx. To Professor Calhoun, the economic interpretation "means simply that the main stream of history consists of those practices that are consistent with the necessity of getting along on this planet, with its limited size and limited resources."

This is far from being the Marxian "economic predestination" in its original form—or as stated in our own time by European socialists like Labriola and Kautsky. Least of all does it resemble the extreme position of Russian communists like Bukharin who claim to be strict Marxians. One could go as far as Calhoun does without being a socialist at all. He admits that much change may consist of "chance or random feelers." As we shall presently see, Bukharin scorns the idea that there is any such thing as chance in history. Free from metaphysical assumptions as Professor Calhoun's statement seems on the surface, and liberal as compared with the position of people like Bukharin, it is still easy to detect a sweeping hypothesis which is neither so obvious nor so innocent as it looks. Is there any such thing as a "main stream" of history, existing objectively and as distinguished from our personal opinions or prejudices as to what is important? This suggests all sorts of questions of basic principle—for example, whether it is permissible to speak of a "general trend" in history which can be applied to various aspects in which we may be interested, and if so whether or not this trend is linear and traceable—but for the moment let us confine ourselves to a practical matter: Have we any sufficient grounds for supposing that the "main stream of history," if any, is of such breadth, force and consistency as to either determine or measure the course of events with any useful degree of certainty? "Useful" in this connection suggests at least two possible aims: first, to interpret observed past happenings in such a way as to shed light on present ones; and second, to give us some cue as to the more problematical future events which cannot be measured, since they have not yet occurred. The first is history, the second prediction.

It is at this point that a well trained and thoroughly experienced historian like Professor Sée parts company with the extreme Marxian economic determinists. A fairly scientific technique has been developed for probing the records—often incomplete, verbal and in no sense quantitative—of things which have undoubtedly happened. But it is only the technique which is scientific, the aims being often merely descriptive, with no intent to predict. To state the probability that past occurrences would repeat themselves—including the degree of probable fidelity to the originals as to details, location, and especially lapse of *time*—we should have to restrict ourselves to those events about which we have exact *quantitative* information.

In the physical sciences, a great many phenomena do repeat themselves with a sufficient uniformity as to details and time intervals to be stated, for practical purposes, in the form of "laws." A scientific law is thus a formula, usually quantitative or mathematical in statement, expressing an observed uniformity, either in such general terms that the assumption of invariability will do no harm, or in terms of the probability that a certain result will appear under given circumstances. Such laws must be abstract; that is, they must be stated in terms which either eliminate or make allowance for the differences between individual observers and objects observed. Even in those physical phenomena where the composition of the materials and the rhythm of their behavior is most nearly uniform, different observers do not get exactly the same results, so that the values stated in the laws are merely the most probable or average ones, each subject to its probable error.

While the strict economic determinists have continued to build upon the eighteenth- and nineteenth-century notions current in popular science, the natural sciences have been put upon a quite different basis. As they have reached downward in size and outward in space for their materials, and stiffened the standards of exactitude, both the unavoidable errors of observation and the variations in phenomena not covered by any simple statement have crept into the formulas. "Cause and effect," in the sense of invariable or inevitable sequence, is a relationship which strictly suits a smaller and smaller percentage of the cases studied. Finally some scientists have taken up the argument that "causation" is merely a mental device for dealing with data, and not to be projected into the data themselves. Thus the eighteenth-century belief in a linear and inevitable course of "progress" or social evolution has fallen into disrepute because it does not express the observed facts; and the same reasoning as applied to biological evolution in the nineteenth century is now as thoroughly discredited. As the latest if not the last straw, Einstein comes along with a proof that even our linear scales of time and space are quite incorrect.

In the seventh chapter of his *Science et philosophie de l'histoire* (Paris, 1928), Professor Sée has traced the development of the concept of evolution, as applied to history, from about 1750 to date. When Darwin published his Origin of Species, Marx was already past forty, and his doctrines had assumed the general form in which we read them today. He had directly inherited the metaphysics and dialectic of Hegel. It would be too long a task for an introduction to trace the eighteenth-century ideas of causation, progress and natural law from Montesquieu and Turgot through Condorcet and many others down to Marx. The notion of a main stream of general causes in history, so strong and coherent that "chance" or "accident" can safely be ignored as of no great consequence in the results, is not at all original with the Marxians. For example, it is stated with perfect clarity in Chapter XVII of Montesquieu's 1734 work on the Greatness and Decline of the Romans. Turgot, Condorcet, and especially the Saint-Simonian socialists, used the scheme of evolutionary economic stages, and the last-mentioned group had a very definite belief in economic determinism.

The main point for us here is that all of these people, including Marx, were dominated by an eighteenth-century view of "causes," "natural laws" and "chance," since largely bowed out of science as a source of confusion and an obstacle to investigation. "Cause" in the old sense had at least a semi-theological significance, inherited from Deism. To regard one event as actually producing another is in fact equivalent to projecting a certain amount of will or intention into the process. This is sometimes covered up by the direct or implied

23

analogy to some simple mechanism which is itself wilfully set up. If the universe itself is treated as such a mechanism, the dilemma is not solved for any curious mind until some popular science explanation is offered for the fact that it is in motion. The assumption that it was always so is a blind alley; for a force at work which can be traced only in a circle is not translatable into everyday experience. It would be perpetual motion, which serves better as a joke than as an explanation. If we carefully refrain from such words as "inevitable," with their veiled imputations of will, we have nothing left but the association of the happenings—uniform to the degree observed, plus or minus the error of observation. The dogma of a chain of inevitable causation in Marxian history is theological rather than scientific. As a practical aid to thought, the feeling that things have "causes" is as useful in modern science as in primitive animism, the human brain being whatever it is; but as people grow more sophisticated they become less inclined to read their feelings into the universe.

A "causal necessity" which turns out to be merely probable, not mandatory, is poor stuff for propaganda. Bucharin, in his *Historical Materialism*, seems particularly annoyed by chance phenomena. Natural law must be deified into "causal law," existing "objectively" both "in nature and in society." The mystery of a religion of materialism is gratuitous, since this particular brand of materialism is permeated with phrases and the vapor of ideas from philosophers long dead who are generally classified as pantheists. These laws of Bukharin's are not merely observed relationships, but self-legislating and self-acting, objective agents of change. One illustration of these irrefragable causal laws (English edition, p. 30) is that "if the productivity of labor increases, prices will fall. . . ." This "law," given without qualifications, is evidently disobeyed with impunity by the mere facts, as shown by many statistical measurements. On an earlier page, the perfect rhythm of cause-and-effect relationships in human society is illustrated with the rather startling opinion: "In capitalist society, crises arise at definite intervals of time, which follow upon industrial booms in as precise a succession as the succession of day and night." Were nature as accommodating as this, we might get rid of the unpredictable element known as "chance"; but unfortunately no such business cycles as here described have been observed in the actual world.

The translation of this Russian communist textbook of "proletarian sociology" into French and English has served the useful purpose of showing where the utter logic of economic determinism leads. "Proletarian science," asserted to be far better and less prejudiced than "bourgeois science," is a curiously syncopated version of eighteenth-century philosophy. Chance or accident in history is disposed of by the assertions that the tossed coin obeys natural laws in falling heads or tails up, though we are unable to predict which, and that an entirely unexpected meeting with a friend is likewise due to "causes," though these are useless to the people concerned because unknown. Chance defined as perfectly lawless phenomena has been a straw man for a long time. Having set him up again while the proletarian audience wasn't looking, Bukharin knocks him over so realistically that one almost forgets his composition.

Chance has no such meaning to the much ridiculed "bourgeois scientists," who make the same reservation Bukharin does as a matter of course, unless they are talking to each other, when it is assumed. In a sufficiently large number of random tosses of a perfectly balanced coin, the ratio of heads to tails would vary around unity. Thus it is said that the probability of heads or of tails in a single such throw is approximately equal. Actual coins are not perfectly balanced. If you select one at random and toss it, the probability —as far as you are concerned—is one out of two that it will fall heads. It may not—the chance of error is quite large in predicting the outcome of any single toss, as observation will prove. At the same time, the probability of getting the expected *ratio* between heads and

26

tails increases with the number of tosses at a rate which need not be discussed here. Though "chance" and "probability" have been used interchangeably above, the word "chance" is often reserved for the phenomena which occur without our having had the opportunity even to calculate the mathematical probability. For example, the badly balanced coin just mentioned will not yield the expected ratios of heads and tails calculated for perfect ones. We could find out by repeated tosses what to expect, but until we do this the difference between this observational probability and the theoretical one is pure chance. It is such by definition, simply because we have no way of knowing what the result will be. There is no suggestion of any freedom of the coin from the laws of dynamics, but only of our ignorance of their operation in this case. Chance in science consists of the undogmatic plain fact that the event so designated is legitimately unexpected. If we cannot predict that it will or will not occur with more than fifty per cent success, it is a chance event, and there is an element of chance in any result which cannot be infallibly predicted.

Darwinism seemed at first to give aid and comfort to those who hoped to reduce the universe to something like the simple positivity of a clock movement. It seemed to explain things in mechanical terms, and thus to reinforce the older notion of progress as a simple and linear trend. By the end of the nineteenth century, variation and chance had regained any ground momentarily lost. As the mechanical explanations became more perfect, they uncovered new problems faster than they solved old ones. Finally it became evident that any mechanical explanation of a life process is merely an explanation of the mechanics so far explored. Whether the word "mechanics" is to cover the whole process depends upon how much we care to loosen up its meaning, and to put things we do not understand at all into formulas, as expressions of probability. The worst blow to the mechanists has been their success in the physical sciences during the past four decades. The old fundamentals have been knocked into a cocked hat, including the atom itself, and the materialists are left without even any certain definition of material. "Postulates" have taken the place of "axioms" in mathematics. Scientific laws have dropped the structural simplicity and rigidity which economic determinists had been trying to force upon the even more refractory social phenomena. The natural sciences themselves have found it convenient to state many relationships in terms of the newer applied probability mathematics, perfected largely in connection with social measurement. Nor have the historical materialists been the leaders in this field.

Most history is unsuitable as a basis for prediction,

for reasons which are not too difficult to grasp. In making forecasts accurate enough for any practical use, some such mathematical technique as regression or correlation has been found indispensable. For example, an economic forecast, which must state the probability that certain units are sufficiently uniform to behave in a rhythmical way throughout a stated period of time, must obviously be expressed in quantitative terms. That such procedure is not a mere useless embroidery of capitalism for the use of speculators can be ascertained by looking into governmental crop-reporting services. Estimating the condition of a crop at any juncture involves the isolation and measurement of those factors which have most affected the final yield in past years, and calculating a ratio between their present observed strength and the probable outcome in such terms as bushels, pounds or bales. This is seen to resemble a compound proportion, in which the accuracy of hitting the unknown term depends upon that of calculating the other three. Where a term is made up of a number of factors, a system of weighting these is indispensable.

For example, to explain the American Revolution in terms of six "causes," without giving any quantitative expressions of their relative importance or making any allowance for error introduced by other factors not considered, may be an aid in thinking about this particular case; but such an explanation is not transferable to another situation. Everyone who has had to deal with the simpler economic predictions in a practical way realizes that they are mere statements of probability, founded on the assumptions that the factors picked out of past situations were really the ones which produced the results, that they are also the ones at work in the present situation, and that proper allowance has been made for the unpredictable circumstances which usually intervene before the appearance of an expected result. Most scientific prediction is a simplified quantitative estimate of the highest present probability. What most of the historical materialists mistake for scientific prediction is rather an attempt, by a cabalistic mixture of logic, metaphysics and rule of thumb, to usurp the rôle of the ancient prophets.

Experience with quantitative measurement should also teach us that the reliability of a social prediction varies inversely with the lapse of time before it is to be fulfilled, and with the number of factors to be measured, weighted and averaged. And the error multiplies in a ratio more like a geometrical one than a simple one. For the same reasons, the applicability of data from a past situation to a present one decreases in like manner as remoteness in time and space increases the probability of a variation in the basic factors at work or their relationship one to another. Thus the probable error in a calculation of the correlation of measurable factors over a short period of time can often be estimated for rough practical purposes; but this error increases very rapidly with the generalization of the forecast in space and time. The non-linearity of the course of social change completely invalidates the Marxian technique of prediction.

Hypotheses as to which forces were of capital importance in a particular historical situation which we are investigating are necessary, and perfectly consistent with sound work. But the assumption that these forces are few in number and always the same ones is a vicious dogma which injects a rhythm into phenomena when it may exist only in the formula. Real scientists find that they must exercise care in order to avoid this in applying even the best methods of one science to the data of another. To give a single example, the use of Fourier mathematical series is indispensable in physics, where the rhythms are harmonic, but is found to assume such a rhythm, and to have a tendency to report it in social data, though it may exist in the set-up of the formula rather than in the events.

The Marxian economic interpretation of history is not to be considered, or criticized, as a method of historical research. It is rather a sociological application of mainly popular history, stated in terms of popular science, to social aims which it is hoped may be achieved through the propaganda. History studies what has occurred—studies it at second hand, to be sure, by means of faulty records. It loses such scientific character as it possesses when it definitely turns to the future. In history, the time of occurrence is a matter of fact, useful in establishing the sequence of events, and often exactly ascertainable. Predictions carried out by reversing this technique fail of any useful purpose if they cannot approximate the time and place as well as the essential details. The only way to establish these begins with a whole set of assumptions about the continuity, in a trend-line which can be accurately plotted, of the infinitely complicated rhythms we think we can detect in the past. This is founded on the further set of assumptions that we have picked the correct items in plotting our trend-line, that it represents the factors, in the proportions, that we think, and that they continue to operate in the same combinations, with the same weights, and without the addition of any important new ones.

Bukharin's statement that "the war" was predicted by the communists is a good illustration. To have more practical significance than fortune-telling, such a forecast must have identified *the* war—that is, a particular one, with its alignment of forces, time of onset, duration, and outcome. He shows that he has nothing of the sort in mind by declaring that "the war" would have come without the killing of the Archduke, and that "subsequent evolution would have been altered so little as not to be essentially changed in any way." This view takes us back to the unripened Montesquieu of 1734, before he had written the mature works which have secured his fame among eighteenth-century *philosophes*. Forecasting in the sane, practical and quantitative sense is a technical process too important in American life for us to stir up much interest in prediction on a cosmic scale, carried out by offhand methods we should reject as insufficient even in the simpler affairs of everyday life.

Only the extremists—not even all the communists—swallow Bukharin's *Historical Materialism* whole. Boris Souvarin, a communist, calls that book a "substitute" (*Ersatz*) for Marxism—a "simplification to the limit." In a 1928 book entitled *Is Marxism Bankrupt?* (*Le Marxisme a-t'il fait faillite?*), the Belgian socialist Vandervelde criticizes extremists like Bukharin for adhering to the narrower views of the *Communist Manifesto* instead of keeping up with the later evolution of Marx's own position. There is a growing tendency to recognize the influence of Engels upon Marx, especially in the later years when the opinions of the former were adjusting themselves rapidly to the newer realities of European life. Vandervelde quotes a remark of Professor E. R. A. Seligman, made years ago, that Marx was himself, during his whole life, the first of the revisionists of Marxism. The ideas of the Bolsheviks seem to Vandervelde "substantially those of Marxism in the beginning, and at that in the simplified and rudimentary forms to which Marx's doctrine was reduced by certain disciples," though later "outgrown and contradicted by Marx himself." Kautsky, though he opposed the revisionism of Bernstein, has shown a capacity for adapting his views to facts, in strong contrast with Bukharin's bitter orthodoxy. Sée, Vandervelde and the sane revisionists generally nevertheless hold to *an* economic interpretation of history, in the sense of treating the economic facts as the capital ones in the stream of events.

If the meaning of the word "interpretation" in scientific work is borne in mind, the historical doctrine divests itself of its prophetic elements and becomes mere common sense—provided always we agree that in practice the economic facts are the easiest to identify and the most convenient to trace. By the interpretation of a process which is new to us and not intelligible by direct observation, says a standard introduction to chemistry, "we mean the explanation of it in terms of phenomena so familiar to us that they do not seem to require any interpretation." An interpretation which we merely use ourselves as a sort of optical instrument to help us where we cannot observe directly is the same thing as a working hypothesis. Once we have discovered some new fact or relationship, and verified it independently of our analogy, the interpretation may become a tool for the *exposition* of our findings to others. A "natural law" itself, since it cannot go into detail about the more or less variable component facts, contains a large element of such exposition or description. It is the great and perhaps unavoidable weakness of popular science that the uninitiated take these "laws" too literally, not realizing that they are largely tools of description, in which the element of hypothesis or analogy covers a multitude of variations and exceptions borne in mind by the working scientist. This is most serious in the case of social data, with their wide and numerous variations, their complicated and irregular rhythms, and with the special difficulty they present in attaining scientific objectivity.

Bukharin to the contrary nevertheless, his class-conscious proletariat is no more a disinterested observer than the bourgeoisie. There is no visible reason why Marxism should be exempt from the influences which distort scientific notions in the hands of the inexpert and prejudiced. Rather would it seem that a history made subsidiary to a scheme for foretelling the future, itself mixed up with an active propaganda for bringing it about, must lack even the usual objectivity.

A charge less commonly made but quite as much to the point is that Marxism suffers to a peculiar degree from an aspect of popular science which is becoming a scourge, if it is not already one. Popular science is not science at all in the vital sense of scientific work, done in chastening contact with the raw material; it is merely the exposition or interpretation mentioned above. But the usefulness of "an explanation . . . in terms of phenomena so familiar . . . that they do not seem to require any interpretation" depends upon the recipient and what he knows already. He may be perfectly *satisfied* with an analogy, bringing in some familiar mechanical process or device, though his ignorance of the principles involved is as blank and utter in the second case as in the original one. For example, an airplane may be "familiar" to one who has no notion whatever of aerodynamics.

In this age of mechanical devices, the world is full of "explanations" and "interpretations" which merely satisfy, like a soothing syrup. Some of the worst social philosophies are concocted by engineers—good technicians as distinguished from scientists—who dream of feeding entirely different data through their formulas. Usually they do not make any actual experiments, but

36

like Korzybski, merely jot down equations and observations which men who have worked with social data, from Cournot to Pearson and Yule, have rejected as unadapted to such materials. Historical materialism has been particularly successful as propaganda. It has satisfied the mass of its customers in terms of popular mechanics and popular science.

Professor Henri Sée is one of the most distinguished of living French historians. Born near Paris September 6, 1864, he entered the University of Paris at the age of nineteen, and remained in residence seven years. Passing his *agrégation* examination with distinction, he was at once marked as one of the select group destined for university teaching and related scholarly careers. His *Doctorat-ès-Lettres*, the State degree which stands in a class by itself in the French educational system, was granted in 1892, his thesis being on the subject: *Louis XI et les villes*. Since 1893, he has been on the faculty of the University of Rennes, with the title of Professor since 1897.

During the thirty-six years since Professor Sée was called to Rennes, he has turned out a mass of detailed, original work in economic history such as few scholars can claim. He has also found time to write some political history and various interpretative works such as the one here presented in English. Besides these, he

37

has written a vast number of articles, both scientific and polemic, and has been associated with many of the most distinguished people in France in the *Lique des droits de l'homme*, an organization to protect personal rights. Incidentally, the standard history of that movement is a product of his pen. History, in the true meaning of the term and as distinguished from philosophizing or popularization about the subject matter, is a profession with a technique which can be mastered only after long and arduous experience with the actual raw materials. It is not learned merely from printed books. Thirty odd years ago, Brittany in particular and northwestern France in general constituted one of the richest regions in Europe in unexplored historical records. These covered the middle ages; they were particularly numerous for the period of European expansion overseas, when Saint-Malo was one of the great ports in the new trade; and they came down through the complicated French-Revolutionary era to the present time. Thanks largely to the efforts of Professor Sée and a group of scholars he has trained or gathered around him, these have now been largely explored. Most of the material has been edited and published, carefully analyzed in books and articles, or arranged for use by those with a taste for what the French very properly call the "science of history."

From the beginning of his career as an historian,

INTRODUCTION TO THE AMERICAN EDITION

Professor Sée has looked beyond the restricted circle of professionals, both in doing his work and in presenting it. In 1901, he published *Les classes rurales et le régime domanial en France au Moyen Age*, still a classic in its field. At that time it was unique to such an extent that it had to be built very largely upon original investigation. This was followed in 1906 by *Les classes rurales en Bretagne du XVIe siècle à la Révolution*, founded almost entirely upon first-hand research. Such books, together with scores of technical articles published in the journals of a half dozen countries, attest the fact that M. Sée has never neglected the professional side of his work. The four volumes of *Cahiers de la senéchaussée de Rennes pour la convocation des États Généraux*, prepared in collaboration with M. André Lesort, appeared between 1909 and 1912. Professor Sée has a number of studies on commercial relations in the Julien Hayem series of *Mémoires et Documents*, of which a dozen volumes have appeared.

One of these papers, *Le commerce de Saint-Malo au XVIIIe Siècle*, is a particularly happy illustration of genuinely scientific methods in the use of difficult source material to get a picture of how trade was carried on during a period long past. This picture was built up almost entirely from the contemporary records and correspondence of business firms—that is, from the data used by those who had carried on the actual commercial operations. Such material is hard to find, and sometimes as difficult to decipher and arrange, but it is the rare sort which brings the historian into direct contact with his facts. The usual, and quite respectable, thing would have been to be satisfied with the records left by the *intendants* of the time, though these government servants omitted many of the most vital economic facts, and were often ignorant of the details of how the businesses were carried on. In this case, only the analysis of account books and correspondence could have disclosed the people, places, goods, prices, organization and methods involved. Even with this kind of exact information in hand, any attempt to generalize it in terms of other firms, regions or periods than the ones observed brings in an element of interpretation or reasoning by analogy. Only a real historical craftsman, who knows all that can be found out about some actual samples, has solid ground to stand upon in surveying the rest.

Since his retirement from active teaching work in 1914, Professor Sée has had more time to finish books and articles already begun, to base new projects upon the accumulated research of years, and to add constantly to his accumulation of materials. Only a few titles can be mentioned here. His books on *Modern Capitalism* and *Economic and Social Conditions in*

INTRODUCTION TO THE AMERICAN EDITION

France during the Eighteenth Century have already appeared in English. A 1928 volume, *Science et philosophie de l'histoire*, is being translated for the present series, and an economic and social history of France, of which the French edition is in press at this writing, is likewise earmarked for translation in the near future. Others of his works are as follows: *Esquisse d'une histoire du régime agraire en Europe aux XVIIIe et XIXe siècles; Les idées politiques en France au XVIIe siècle; L'évolution de la pensée politique en France au XVIIIe siècle; L'évolution commerciale et industrielle de la France sous l'ancien régime;* and *La vie économique de la France sous la monarchie censitaire (1815–1848)*. Space is wanting to mention in detail articles which have been printed in many countries, including several in the American Historical Review and the Encyclopædia of the Social Sciences.

A book on the economic interpretation of history by an historian of Professor Sée's professional standing would have attracted attention even in a period less vitally concerned with the subject matter than the present one. Its interest is heightened by the fact that he is himself a socialist. This fact is merely mentioned in passing, in the introduction of one of the few books in this field which can be read carefully without yielding any indication of the author's personal views. He is so completely the honest and competent historian that even those who think he has handled a socialist doctrine with a great deal of freedom have found little to say in criticism.

M. M. KNIGHT
University of California

PART I

GENESIS AND CHARACTER
OF THE MARXIAN DOCTRINE

CHAPTER I

GENESIS OF THE DOCTRINE
THE "COMMUNIST MANIFESTO"

THE materialistic conception of history—the doctrine that economic phenomena determine all other manifestations of the history of human society—is really the work of Karl Marx and his friend and collaborator Friedrich Engels, although they may have borrowed certain elements from other thinkers.

It will be well, therefore, to recall briefly how this doctrine gradually took shape in their minds. Let us note to begin with that Marx was at first an enthusiastic student of the philosophy of Hegel and was equally familiar with that of Kant. Thus Woltmann has grounds for saying that Marxian philosophy and the materialistic conception of history have their roots for the most part in German philosophy.[1]

When Marx became manager of the *Rheinische Zeitung* in 1842 his ideas do not seem to have differed greatly from those of the radical younger Hegelians.[2] In a letter written in 1837 or 1838, however, he already uses the materialistic dialectic.[3] Economic questions engage his attention more and more, and in the

45

Rheinische Zeitung we see him criticizing directly the legalistic school, which he reproaches for considering all legal institutions as the result of a long evolution.

After the suppression of the *Rheinische Zeitung* Marx came to Paris, where he entered into close contact with both the exiled German communists and the French socialists.[4] In 1844 he founded the *Deutsch-französische Jahrbücher* in collaboration with Arnold Ruge, from which we may deduce the evolution of his ideas at the time. He began to show clearly why the revolution of the fourth estate, the proletarist, is necessary: it is because economic considerations take precedence over political questions.[5] He believed that the French Revolution was important not so much because it had freed political forces as because it had shaken the economic foundation on which the political super-structure had been erected.

Although Marx had at first been a follower of Hegel and had shared the ideas of the radical young Hegelians, he had already fallen away from them in 1844, as may be seen from his *Criticism of the Hegelian Philosophy of Law.*[6] He had at this time formed a clear idea of the materialistic conception of history, and in the preface to his *Critique of Political Economy*, published in 1859,[7] he sets forth the conclusions at which he had arrived in 1844:

GENESIS OF THE DOCTRINE

"In their productive activities men form certain necessary and inevitable relations independent of their own
will. These relations correspond to a certain degree of
development in their material productive forces. The sum
total of these relations forms the economic structure of
society, the real foundation on which the legal and political superstructure is erected, and to which certain definite
social forms of consciousness correspond. . . . It is not
man's consciousness that determines his existence, but his
social existence that determines his consciousness."

There comes a time, he adds, when the productive
forces of society are in contradiction with legal relations, that is, with the property system. This system
becomes an obstacle: "The shifting of the economic
foundation sooner or later ruins the whole of the enormous superstructure. In all upheavals the two elements must be distinguished. At the same time, productive relationships superior to the existing ones do
not replace these until the material basis has been
developed in the new society." [8]

The Marxian concept at this time emerges still more
clearly from the influence of Feuerbach.[9] Karl Marx
had at first conceived a great enthusiasm for the ideas
of this brilliant philosopher, but he fell away from
them and reproached Feuerbach for not having seen
that religious sentiment itself is a product of society:
his sensualist conception is after all, at bottom, only
an idealistic doctrine.[10]

47

Friedrich Engels asserts that Karl Marx is the real inventor of the materialistic conception of history and that he himself cannot in any way claim a share in it. May it not be, however, that he is too modest? In any case, his admirable description of the situation of English laborers, *The Condition of the Working Class in England in 1844*, which appeared in 1845,[11] went a long way towards giving a solid basis to the doctrine.[12] With great clearness and precision, he gives a vivid description of the industrial revolution, and shows how this revolution brings about the "proletarization of the workingman." When free competition prevails, hostility and conflicts arise on all sides, and two great enemy camps face each other: the bourgeoisie and the proletariat. Engels gives a precise definition of the "bourgeoisie": it includes all property holders, the landed aristocracy as well as the manufacturers.

The bourgeoisie care for nothing but profit, and are inspired by no humanitarian sentiment, as shown by the new Poor Law, which Engels paints in sombre colors. As industrial and capitalist concentration becomes more and more marked, the property holders will be reduced to a very small minority, and the "reserve army" of workmen will become more and more numerous. Social war is therefore inevitable. It is in reality the Marxian doctrine in its entirety that appears already in Engel's impressive work. Class conflict is defined with the utmost precision; there exist only two classes, or rather two economic abstractions: capital and labor. "Der Fabrikant," says Engels, "ist *das Kapital*, der Arbeiter ist *die Arbeit*." ("The manufacturer is capital, the laborer is labor".)[13]

These are the concrete elements which came to reinforce the philosophic doctrine of economic materialism.[14] It is only natural that Marx should have separated himself from the sentimental socialists, whom he stigmatized as Utopians. Among them he included nearly all the French theorists, in particular Proudhon, against whom in 1847 he directed his virulent but somewhat confused pamphlet *The Poverty of Philosophy*.[15]

Marx endeavors to show that property is not an abstract conception, as the legalists and metaphysicians claim, but that it depends directly on modes of production.[16] He asserts that his doctrine alone is genuinely scientific. In reality, as Andler shows,[17] it is not so original as he thought. He had profited much by the works of theorists who had preceded him, such as Proudhon (whom he attacked so bitterly), Sismondi, Friedrich List, and in particular Pecqueur, who in his work entitled *Des intérêts du commerce* had strongly emphasized the importance of industrial concentration, the effects of machinery and the proletarization of the middle classes.[18] Marx, however, displays more capacity for synthesis,[19] a reasoning power and an impetuousness which obscure the work of other thinkers who are not less original but who lack his fire.

However it may be, all this agitation of ideas resulted in the celebrated *Communist Manifesto* of 1847, in which the thesis of economic materialism appeared in broad daylight.

It is a significant fact that this manifesto of conflict [20] opens not with a statement of principles but with an historical survey, in which the materialistic conception of history is clearly and sharply defined. In a certain way this doctrine is crystallized in the conception of class conflict: "The history of all society down to our own time has been merely the history of class struggles."

In every epoch this antagonism crops out, but it is the characteristic feature of the "era of the bourgeoisie" to have simplified class conflicts by allowing only two hostile classes to subsist, the bourgeoisie and the proletariat.

The Manifesto then gives a vivid sketch of the genesis of this era of the bourgeoisie. Great discoveries open up a vast new field of action to this class, and the development of capitalism results in large scale industries. Thus the modern bourgeoisie appears as the product of a long development, of a series of revolutions in the modes of production and exchange. The bourgeois class has played a genuinely revolutionary part, "has trodden under foot feudal, patriarchal and idyllic relations," and has practised "naked, shameless, direct, brutal exploitation." One of its most striking characteristics is to have given "a cosmopolitan character to production and consumption in every country."

Today, however, "the productive forces at the disposal of the bourgeoisie no longer serve to strengthen the position of bourgeois property. On the contrary, they have enormously outgrown the narrow shell of such ownership, which therefore hampers them. . . ." Hence the bourgeoisie has forged weapons which will be its own destruction, and has also produced the men to wield these weapons, that is, the proletariat.

The proletarian class has not ceased to expand, whereas the lesser bourgeoisie—small manufacturers, merchants, people retired on small incomes, artisans and peasant land holders—is dying out. It lacks capital and its means of production are insufficient. It is destined to lose its economic independence.

At first the workingmen fought the enemies of the bourgeoisie, that is, the vestiges of absolute monarchy and the great landed proprietors. Now, however, they are rising against the bourgeoisie itself, which "is asking history to flow backwards." The proletariat can be seen organizing itself more and more into a class.

Thus historical evolution itself calls on all the unpropertied to work for the destruction of the method of appropriation current down to our time. The fall of the bourgeoisie and the victory of the proletariat are inevitable. The *Manifesto* contains this characteristic passage, addressed to the bourgeoisie:

> "Have not your very ideas arisen from bourgeois conditions of production and property? What is your legal system but the will of your class made into a law for everybody—a will whose essential character and direction are determined by economic conditions of your own class's existence?"

It will be seen that this vigorous *Communist Manifesto* already contains in substance the whole Marxian program of social and political agitation. In their later works Marx and Engels simply developed and defined the ideas already so powerfully expressed in the *Manifesto*.

What was appearing, as Antonio Labriola suggests,[21] was a new conception of history, one destined above all to have practical consequences since it sought to demonstrate that the communist system was bound to triumph: "Society will pass on to communism by virtue of the inherent laws of its development." [22]

CHAPTER II

DEFINITION AND CHARACTER
OF THE DOCTRINE

WE are now in a position to form a definite idea of what Marx and Engels understood by the materialistic conception of history. Their theory is that economic phenomena determine all other historical facts and make it possible to explain them. The economic foundation (*unterbau*) has always determined all legal and political institutions, all intellectual facts such as those of literature and art, all that superstructure (*oberbau*) which up to that time had been exclusively considered by historians. These latter had been blind to all save ideology, whereas this ideology was merely the product of the fundamental phenomena related to the satisfaction of the essential human needs of subsistence and reproduction.

It is true, Marx and Engels admitted, that all these superficial or ideological phenomena have a certain interest and importance, but especially as manifestations of the *unterbau*. In reality the visible facts of history merely reveal the economic structure. Wars, diplomatic events, religious developments, even intellectual transformations themselves, can be explained only by economic life. Political conflicts are only the superficial manifestations of the class conflicts that have existed at every epoch of history. It is true that superior individuals have been able to play more prominent rôles, but in reality they have been only unconscious marionettes acting out a drama of whose real significance they were ignorant. Labriola says on this subject: [1]

"Martin Luther, like the other great reformers, his contemporaries, never knew as we know today, that the Reformation was but an episode in the development of the Third Estate and an economic revolt of the German nation against the exploitation of the Papal Court. He was what he was, as an agitator and a politician, because he was wholly taken up with the belief which made him see, in the class movement which gave an impulse to the agitation, a return to true Christianity and a divine necessity in the vulgar course of events."

Marx, Engels and their followers believed that the materialistic conception was really scientific, and that by using it the *laws* of historical evolution could be worked out. Very significant in this connection is the preface written by Friedrich Engels to the 1885 edition of the *Dix-huit brumaire de Louis Bonaparte:* [2]

"Marx was the first to discover the great law of historical movement, namely that all historic conflicts waged in the political, religious, philosophic or any other ideologic field are in reality merely the more or less definite translation of conflicts waged between social classes, and that the existence of these classes, as well as the conflicts between them, is determined by the degree of development in their economic condition, by their mode of production and by the method of exchange derived from it."

He adds that "this law, in history, is as important as the law of the transformation of energy in the mathematical sciences." Labriola [3] also considers that "critical communism foresees the future because what it says and predicts must inevitably happen by the immanent necessity of history. . . ."

Later, however, Engels was to make considerable modifications in the doctrine. Neither Marx nor himself, he says, ever claimed that the economic substructure was the only important phenomenon. It is of course the base, but all that constitutes the superstructure, that is, the political forms of class conflict, legal forms, political and philosophical theories, and religious conceptions themselves, also influence historical events and even economic phenomena; there is constant action and reaction.[4] It may be, however, that in the light of experience Engels had considerably modified his own views, perhaps without fully realizing it. In any case, Marx's doctrine is the one explained above, and it is so interpreted by most of his followers such as Labriola and Kautsky.[5] Furthermore, two letters from Engels dated October 27, 1890, and January 25, 1894,[6] clearly show that in his view it is really the economic phenomena that underlie political and legal phenomena and even religious and philosophical concepts, which are "merely economic reflections"; the economic evolution always exerts the "dominant and decisive influence." While he does not completely ignore the part played by chance and by individuals, yet "the necessity which shows itself through all the play of chances always turns out to be the economic necessity." If Napoleon had not existed, "another would have taken his place." Science depends above all on the "*condition* and the requirements of technique." [7]

CHAPTER III

APPLICATIONS OF THE THEORY

CAN history be regarded as an exact science? This is a question which we are not called upon to discuss for the moment;[1] but it is quite evident that when the *Communist Manifesto* appeared Engels and Marx were still novices in historical investigation. The field was new to them.[2] On a certain number of contemporary events which they had been able to observe, and which moreover they had observed with great insight, they built up their theory.

It was more particularly in later years that they endeavored to control this theory, relying less on the study of the remoter past than on that of very recent events. In 1850 Marx published *La lutte des classes en France de 1848 à 1850* (The Class Struggle in France, 1848–1850), in which he vividly characterized the various classes in France and tried to prove that all the political events of that time were determined by the conflict between these classes. His study would tend to show, moreover, that there were not merely two classes in conflict (that is, the bourgeoisie and the proletariat), but that financiers, manufacturers, merchants and the lower middle class had different and usually conflicting interests. This is also the impression left by *The Eighteenth Brumaire of Louis Bonaparte*. In the proletariat, moreover, a distinction must be made between industrial workers and agricultural laborers, but on this point Marx's ideas seem to be more or less confused. He had no very clear view of the social and economic status of the peasant classes. "Bonaparte," he tells us, "represents a class, and even the most numerous class, of bourgeois society, that of the small peasant proprietors." He adds that these peasants did not, properly speaking, form a class, since although they were subject to similar economic conditions they did not constitute a coherent and self-conscious whole. Although many peasants revolted against the government at the time of the *coup d'état*, it was because they had been ruined by mortgages, had fallen into the ranks of the proletariat, and thus no longer had identical interests with the bourgeoisie. He should, however, have made a thorough investigation to determine the category to which these insurgent peasants belonged. This question has not yet been cleared up, and it was much more obscure immediately after the events, when Marx wrote about them. Although vigorous and clear-sighted, his two essays on the subject arrive at more or less hypothetical conclusions.

In this same work he informs us that "industry and commerce, the occupations of the middle class, must flourish under a strong government as in a hothouse." This aphorism may be true, but it requires demonstration.

It was also in the light of his doctrine of social classes that Marx described the revolutionary events of Central Europe in letters sent to the New York *Daily Tribune* in 1851 and 1852. These have been published in a volume under the title *Revolution and Counter-Revolution; or Germany in 1848.*[3] This is really a work of the highest order. With great force Marx depicted economic and social Germany since 1815. He described the conditions of the various classes, showing how Germany differed from England and France, because of the persistence of the feudal aristocracy and the maintenance of seigniorial rights over the peasants. Large scale industries were still in their infancy and the lower middle class occupied a very important place. It was only the industrial progress after 1840 that brought the bourgeoisie into conflict with the old feudal group.

Revolution was inevitable, and would have occurred even without the French insurrection of February 1848, because all classes, except the higher nobility and the civilian and military officials, were hostile to the governments. The opposition formed such a heterogeneous mass, however, that the revolution was bound to fail. In April, 1848, the victorious upper middle class joined the feudal nobility to combat "the mass of the people and the small merchants." In May, 1849, the insurrection became general in Southern and Western Germany, but the "real combatants" were the workmen, although the peasants joined them, and the lower middle class, the small merchants, claimed to lead the movement. The incapacity and cowardice of the latter, however, brought about the defeat of the insurrection in July, and the Parliament of Frankfort, which had been unwilling to take the lead, also disappeared. The revolution was over.[4] It must be admitted that in this brilliant treatise Marx, while emphasizing class conflict and the economic element, does not ignore the other factors, especially in dealing with the Austrian revolution. He shows a remarkable ability to grasp reality.[5]

At the same time, in 1850, Engels was studying the Peasant War of 1525 [6] by way of adducing examples to justify the materialistic conception of history. He showed that the religious factor must be relegated to the background, and endeavored to bring out the reciprocal action of the several social classes. It was a brilliant essay, founded not on personal research, which alone is really scientific, but on the judicious use of the best works which had appeared up to that time.

Later on, in a really scientific work, *Capital*, Marx appeals to history in explaining "capitalist accumulation." [7] It cannot be denied that all this part of his work shows extensive knowledge and often great acumen. He is seeking, moreover, for a confirmation of the ideas which he had already set forth in the *Communist Manifesto*. This is clear from Chapter **XXVI**: "The capitalistic economic order is born from the loins of the feudal economic order; the dissolution of one freed the constituent elements of the other." [8] Karl Marx wanted to prove that before the wage earner could triumph the serfs had to be freed and the laboring classes then deprived of their means of production. In Chapter **XXVII**, one of the best documented, he shows us how the expropriation of the peasant population came about in England. This is a vigorous and truthful picture on the whole, and more accurate than the following chapter, in which Marx describes the "bloody legislation against the expropriated." He absolutely mistakes the real character of the legislation and administration of the Tudors, who exercised a veritable tutelary patronage over the working classes. This is an error which can obviously be explained by the inadequacy of historical research at the time when Marx was writing, but it is due also to the *a priori* notion that economic phenomena determine all other historical facts. All recent historical studies agree that the monarchical power, still very strong under the Tudors, curbed the usurpations of the landed aristocracy, which were given free rein only after the revolution of 1688, when the gentry got all public authority into its hands. Nor must it be forgotten that capitalism was far from being triumphant in the sixteenth century or even in the seventeenth. The system of small industries still prevailed.[9]

In the chapters dealing with the "genesis of the capitalist farmer" and the "reaction of the agricultural revolution on industry,"[10] there is certainly much truth, and many of the views are profound and illuminating. In Marx's treatise, however, all these transformations are presented too simply, not to say too naïvely, and run too smoothly. The truth is much more complex and less rational. We carry away the impression that we are dealing with an *a priori* theory which directs the entire procedure.

One of the best parts of this telling piece of work is the chapter which describes the "genesis of the industrial capitalist."[11] There are splendid pages on the results of the great discoveries, on the exploitation of the wealth of the New World, on the nature of the colonial system, and on the merciless exploitation of the native population, which paved the way for the exploitation of white workingmen in England. "In fact," concludes Marx, "the veiled slavery of the wage-earners in Europe needed, for its pedestal, slavery pure and simple in the new world." [12] This is a powerful picture, some parts of which history has since been able to retouch, but which remains true as a whole.

It is to be noted moreover that although in *Capital* Marx employs the materialistic conception of history, the book is not in the least intended to prove the solidity of the doctrine. The author considers this to be an established truth, or in any case an obvious one. *Capital* was intended to support the collectivist thesis, to prove that capital had been constituted from the spoliation of workingmen, and that it continued to function thanks to the *surplus value*, which cheated the workman out of a large part of the product of his labor. In reality, however, at the basis of the entire Marxian doctrine is to be found the materialistic conception of history, and all who have made a serious study of the doctrine are agreed on this point. [13]

CHAPTER IV

A PRIORI NATURE OF THE MATERIALISTIC CONCEPTION

WE are beginning to realize that Marxian determinism was not the result of an experimental study of concrete history, but of an *a priori* conception. It was also a weapon in the hands of social agitators such as Marx and Engels, and we shall see what a practical and effective weapon it made. They were not disinterested scholars solely occupied in searching for the truth.

Labriola makes a fairly true statement of the case:

"Our doctrine . . . was born on the battlefield of communism. It assumes the appearance of the modern proletariat on the political stage, and it assumes that alignment upon the origins of our present society which has permitted us to reconstruct in a critical manner the whole genesis of the bourgeoisie. It is a doctrine revolutionary from two points of view; because it has found the reasons and the methods of development of the proletarian revolution which is in the making, and because it proposes to find the causes and the conditions of development of all other social revolutions which have taken place in the past, in the class antagonisms which arrived at a certain critical

64

point, by reason of the contradiction between the forms of production and the development of the producing forces. And this is not all. In the light of this doctrine what is essential in history is summed up in these critical moments." [1]

Although it is difficult to reconstruct with absolute precision the processes of thought which led Marx and Engels to set up their materialistic conception of history, at least the influence of German metaphysics on the genesis of the doctrine cannot be denied—in particular that of the Hegelian dialectic. [2]

It is essential therefore to recall the characteristics of Hegel's logic. [3] According to him there exists in every affirmation a contradiction, an antinomy. The negation of a proposition leads to a superior affirmation, so that, to quote MacTaggart, one of Hegel's followers: "thought advances by steering now in one direction, now another, like a sailing vessel tacking against a head wind." Hegel holds that, in its dialectic progress, knowledge not only loses nothing on the way, but carries along all that it has acquired and becomes enriched and condensed in itself. In reality, it has been remarked that by double negation we return simply to affirmation. The famous dialectic, as Hoeffding says, is a sleight-of-hand performance. Hegel applies dialectic deduction to reality: nature is itself the proof of the dialectic. All sciences must use the same method.

This dialectic seems still more difficult to apply to history than to the natural sciences, for as Meyerson justly observes, "the concept of reality at which Hegel arrives, his perfect timeless universe, excludes absolutely any notion of *becoming*." Troeltsch also shows that it is no *a priori* conception of concrete history that Hegel sets up; he keeps himself clear of time, so to speak, when he endeavors to "rationalize" history and to consider it in its logical aspect (*logisieren*).[4]

It seems unquestionable that Marx was inspired by the Hegelian dialectic,[5] but, as Troeltsch also points out,[6] he has impregnated it with revolutionary spirit, with naturalism and above all with the economic conception (*oekonomisierung*). Thus Hegelianism, which on its right wing served to support the absolutism of the State, on its left arrived at the concept of class war. This concept, says Troeltsch, is the consequence of Marxian logic, and the materialistic conception of history is therefore also a product of it.[7]

It is true that Marx denied being a true disciple of Hegel. In a preface to the second edition of *Capital* he says: "My dialectic method is not only different from the Hegelian, but is its direct opposite. To Hegel, the life-process of the human brain, i. e., the process of thinking, which, under the name of "the Idea," he even transforms into an independent subject, is the demiurgos of the real world, and the real world is only the external, phenomenal form of "the Idea." With me, on the contrary, the ideal is nothing else than the material world reflected by the human mind, and translated into forms of thought." He admits, however, that "the mystification which dialectic suffers in Hegel's hands, by no means prevents him from being the first to present its general form of working in a comprehensive and conscious manner. With him it is standing on its head. It must be turned right side up again, if you would discover the rational kernel within the mystical shell." While mystic logic suits the propertied classes, rational logic is critical and revolutionary, "because it includes in its comprehension and affirmative recognition of the existing state of things, at the same time also, the recognition of the negation of that state, of its inevitable breaking up. . . ." He adds: "The contradictions inherent in the movement of capitalist society impress themselves upon the practical bourgeois most strikingly in the changes of the periodic cycle, through which modern industry runs, and whose crowning point is the universal crisis."

It will be seen that the Marxian dialectic is the legitimate offspring of the Hegelian. It animates all of Marx's books, and in particular *Capital*. Everywhere we find the idea of contradictions and antagonisms resolving themselves into a new and superior form. In this connection there is a very characteristic passage in Chapter **XXXII** of *Capital:*

> "The capitalist mode of appropriation, the result of the capitalist mode of production, produces capitalist private property. This is the first negation of individual private property, as founded on the labour of the proprietor. But capitalist production begets, with the inexorability of a law of Nature, its own negation. *It is the negation of negation.*[8] This does not re-establish private property for the producer, but gives him individual property based on the acquisitions of the capitalist era: i. e., on co-operation and the possession in common of the land and of the means of production."

In *The Poverty of Philosophy* of 1847, Marx reproaches Proudhon not for having used the Hegelian dialectic, which he himself had taught him, but for having misunderstood and misapplied it, and for having, in the *Contradictions économiques*, stated the *thesis* and *antithesis* fairly well while missing the *synthesis:*

> "Hegel," he says, "has no problems to put. He has only dialectic. M. Proudhon has of the dialectic of Hegel nothing but the language. His dialectic movements for him is the dogmatic distinction of good and evil." [9]

When we attempt to solve the problem of eliminating the bad side "we interrupt the dialectic movement." [10]

Hegel's dialectic is also responsible for the Marxian

68

conception of sudden transformations, of visible shifting of scenery, of *catastrophies*, and also of the clearly-defined historical periods which Marx loves to describe. This also explains the lack of shading, and that *rationalization* of history which often ignores real facts, precisely because they would not fit into those rational categories so dear to Marxian doctrine as well as to Hegelian logic.[11]

At the same time, the use of this dialectic allowed Marx to disguise certain contradictions in his theory, as Eduard Bernstein has clearly pointed out.[12] On the one hand, Marx believed that the socialist regime would come as the necessary consequence of the maturing of the forces of production developing in bourgeois society, and on the other, he was unwilling to abandon the Blanquist idea of expropriation for the benefit of the proletariat carried out by a political coup (*Putsch*). This is an obvious contradiction, a "dualism," which as clear a mind as Marx's would doubtless have repudiated if the Hegelian dialectic had not accustomed him to tolerate such contradictions, common enough in the logic of the man who had been his first master. Bernstein is more or less justified in stating that the solid part of Marxism is the part which does not depend on this dialectic, which, he says in an almost untranslatable phrase "schielt nach Wahrheit, wie das Irrlicht nach Erleuchtung." [13]

It is therefore no paradox to claim that the materialistic conception of history is largely an *a priori* conception, metaphysical and in a sense idealistic.[14]

If it seems at times a cheap version of the truth, it is because Marx sees things almost exclusively as an economist. He may criticize the orthodox economists with force and even virulence, and show the weakness of their arguments or the feebleness of their logic. At the same time he agrees with them that laws can be determined—not eternal laws perhaps, but the scentific laws of economic phenomena.[15] This is an illusion which it will be very difficult to uproot. Political economy can observe facts, recognize certain tendencies and formulate hypotheses, but is it more reasonable to speak of the laws of economics than of the laws of history? The more political economy becomes impregnated with history and the historical method, the better it will understand that it cannot aspire to determine laws analogous to those of the physical sciences.[16] Even as an economist, moreover, Marx is not the detached scholar seeking only to discover the truth; as has been aptly remarked, he is also Marx the man of action, Citizen Marx.[17]

At the same time, however, Marx has a very acute sense of concrete facts, and a remarkable aptitude for grasping historical events in their most vivid aspect, and this is what constitutes his originality and strength. It is true that he twists these events more or less to suit his own ideas, but not altogether; in many respects he has the scientific spirit.[18] For this reason the materialistic conception of history is not a mere intellectual game, a sleight-of-hand trick, such as the Hegelian philosophy is so often capable of performing. Thus, in spite of many errors, it contains a large element of truth, and when all is said and done it must be admitted that it has not only been a prodigious means of action but a powerful stimulus to the advance of historical studies.

Benedetto Croce very justly observes that Karl Marx has contributed much to show history under a new light. Whoever becomes imbued with Marx's spirit "is like a short-sighted man who has provided himself with a good pair of spectacles: he sees quite differently, and many mysterious shadows reveal their exact shape. . . ." [19]

It is because they tried to probe economic facts that Marx and Engels had a more profound view of things than even a great mind like Carlyle, who placed moral considerations first. In this connection one should read *Past and Present*, written in 1843. No one has depicted with more poetic force the wretchedness of laborers in England and the selfishness of its aristocracies, the industrial aristocracy as well as the idle gentry; no one has more virulently stigmatized the worship of Mammon. His ideal is found in the past, however, rather than in the future; he draws an idyllic picture of the administration of the Abbey of St. Edmundsbury. It is true that Carlyle shows the necessity of legislative intervention in industrial matters and favors inspection of labor and public education at the charge of the State. He wished to convince the British nation, so conservative by nature, that it is imperatively necessary to change an abominable state of affairs. He holds nevertheless that liberty and equality, the non-aristocracies, are as impossible as the false aristocracies. For him the aristocracy and the priesthood are the vital elements of all society. This extreme individualist sees salvation only in the hero, the true hero, who will combat selfishness and the worship of Mammon, and not the hero who fights bloody battles against foreign nations.[20]

CHAPTER V

SCIENCE AND UTOPIA

ALL of the foregoing considerations incline us to think that neither the materialistic conception of history as Karl Marx conceived it, nor the socialist theory to which it gave birth (or which perhaps inspired it), is so purely scientific in its nature as its creator believed.

To take the question of his socialism, was not Marx somewhat mistaken when he so brutally and haughtily opposed the so-called *utopian* socialism of his predecessors, and in particular that of the French theorists? The first battery he brought to bear on them was Hegelian logic. "What has saved Germany from the metaphysical and fantastic notions of Lamennais, Proudhon, Saint-Simon and Fourier," he declares, "is the logic of Hegel." Now this logic, as we have seen, is pure idealism.

It is true that Marx claims precisely the contrary, since he bases his entire system on *reality*, but when all is said and done he is not a pure scientist, free from all metaphysical leanings. As Woltmann justly points out,[1] his theory of history is still *teleological*, and preserves many traces of idealistic German philosophy. In a word, there is in Marx something of the metaphysician, something of the idealist and even something of the ideologist.[2]

He severely reproaches some of the French writers, and in particular Proudhon, for invoking the sentiment or the idea of justice. He considers this to be a serious error, both because the notion of justice changes with the economic organization, and because for eighteen hundred years this famous justice has been appealed to in vain. It must be noted, however, that these statements were made at the beginning of his career.[3] Did not Marx's ideas on these matters change?

Be that as it may, he himself appealed to the sentiment of justice and humanity. To all his friends, to all those who approached him, Karl Marx gave the impression of being a good man, fine, sensitive, and full of compassion for the weak.[4] D. Riazonov is correct in asserting that Marx was not only "a great genius," a thinker of the first order and an ardent revolutionary, but that "he was also a man to whom nothing human was without interest. Although his manner was sometimes rough, it concealed an infinite affection for all toilers and for all the oppressed." [5] Witness the eloquent and moving pages of *Capital*,[6] in which he describes and stigmatizes the impure sources of capitalism: "If money, according to Augier, 'comes into the world with a congenital blood-stain on one cheek,' capital comes dripping from head to foot, from every pore, with blood and dirt."

Is it only to ensure the triumph of a law of history (which in any case he holds to be inevitable) that he advises workingmen to organize, and that at the end of the *Communist Manifesto* he utters his famous battle cry: "Workingmen of all countries, unite!" Is it not also in order to bring about a more just society?[7] Does he not intuitively feel that in order to be possible and effective every great movement must not only appeal to material interests, but must also arouse the enthusiasm of those who have risen up to carry it on to victory?[8]

If Marx had been a pure scientist, and therefore indifferent to the practical application of his ideas, and if at the same time he had believed in the infallibility of the law of history which he had formulated, he would calmly have waited in his study until the predicted event came to pass. As a matter of fact, he did nothing of the sort, but followed with passionate interest the spread and success of socialist propaganda throughout the world.[9] Woltmann attributed this contradiction to the opposition between the revolutionary and the dialectic tendencies: "In their hearts

75

the founders of Marxism are full of the sentiment of liberty and justice, but their heads obey the dialectic of Hegel." [10]

This is very justly observed: the materialistic conception of history does not derive exclusively from the philosophy of Hegel or the study of social phenomena, but also from the revolutionary spirit. Marx and Engels attribute very great importance to the *will*, though not so much that of the individual as that of social groups. For this reason, they attach great value to propaganda among the proletariat.[11]

As a matter of fact the doctrine has been a marvelous weapon for revolutionists, and has powerfully contributed to the organization of the working class. This result is at first sight surprising, since Marx had represented the arrival of the socialist regime as inevitable. But we must remember that this revolution was ceasing to be a distant and more or less problematical possibility, and was becoming an event to be realized certainly and soon.[12] What a stimulus to action![13] Karl Marx announced the arrival of the Messiah. From many points of view does he not indeed appear in the guise of a prophet?

CHAPTER VI

HAVE MARX'S PREDICTIONS BEEN REALIZED?

IT must be admitted that these predictions have been but imperfectly realized. In the three quarters of a century since the appearance of the *Communist Manifesto*, industrial and capitalistic concentration have progressed, it is true, but much more slowly and less generally than Marx predicted.

The criticisms of the German socialist Eduard Bernstein [1] deserve also to be taken into consideration. He shows that the number of persons participating in capital as shareholders in stock companies has been increasing instead of diminishing. It is true that since shares are anonymous the statistics are not always as convincing as we could wish, but it is a significant fact that in England the number of families with an income of 150 to 1000 pounds rose from 300,000 in 1850 to 990,000 in 1881. There was therefore a growth of the number of property holders out of all proportion to the increase in the population.[2] Bernstein further remarks that the number of small and medium size undertakings, especially the latter, has also increased rather than diminished. It is true that the number of larger concerns has increased even more, but not at the expense of the small ones. In industry new specialties are continually being created, and often engendered by the very development of the great undertakings; finishing work is often carried on by medium sized and small concerns. In commerce the concentration is still less marked than in industry, in spite of the creation of great department and food stores.[3]

These are the interesting observations of Bernstein. It is a fact that industrial and commercial concentration has come about much more slowly than Marx had assumed. Nor can it be said that "time has nothing to do with the matter," for it is anything but a negligible factor. It seems, however, that Bernstein himself underestimates the extent of the concentration. We note a relative diminution in the number of small concerns employing a limited number of workmen, and a significant increase in the number of great ones which employ from 50 to 100 operatives. The concentration of financial capitalism is equally unquestionable—even more marked than that of industrial capitalism. This is perhaps the most important phenomenon, in spite of Kautsky's views to the contrary.[4] Since the world war this concentration has been accentuated, involving the impoverishment of officials and persons living on incomes, which in a country like France constitutes a notable percentage of the middle classes.[5] In Germany the middle class is still worse off than in France. It is true that industry and commerce require more and more the services of technicians, who to some extent fill the gaps left in this middle class, but these experts are only wage earners, however much they may lead the "bourgeois" life.

Marx had also predicted the disappearance of the small peasant land holdings. Relying on the example of England, he believed them to be incompatible with industrial concentration. This system is an intermediate stage indispensable for the development of agriculture, but the "causes which bring about its downfall show its limitations. These causes are: Destruction of rural house industries, which form its normal supplement, as a result of the development of great industries; a gradual deterioration and exhaustion of the soil subjected to this cultivation; usurpation, on the part of the great landlords, of the community lands, which form everywhere the second supplement of small peasants' property and alone enable them to keep cattle; competition, either of plantation systems or of great agricultural enterprises carried out on a capitalist scale. Improvements of agriculture, which on the one hand bring about a fall in the prices of the products of the soil, and on the other require greater investments and more diversified material conditions of production, also contribute toward this end, as they did in England during the first half of the eighteenth century." [6]

The small peasant property, added Marx, is ruined by usury and taxes; furthermore, the capital expenditure incurred in purchasing the land "withdraws this capital from cultivation." The dissipation of means of production, the waste of human power and the gradual impoverishment of the soil are fatal to the small peasant property.[7]

It is not difficult to discover that the evolution of the small holding has not followed the trend predicted by Marx.[8] In countries where it is firmly established, such as France and Western Germany, it has suffered no check, and the condition of the peasant landholders is far from growing worse. In the Scandinavian countries, especially in Denmark, the peasant owner is very prosperous. In the Austrian monarchy the revolution of 1848 freed such property from "the very last vestiges of feudalism." [9] In Russia the principal result of the revolution of 1917 has been the annihilation of noble property holding and the consolidation of peasant ownership.[10] In Poland, Rumania, Bulgaria and Jugoslavia agrarian reforms have recently been carried out tending to limit the great holdings and to extend the system of peasant ownership. Finally, capitalism is far from having strongly imposed itself upon agricultural production, which, depending on the most stable element of all, the soil, has for the most part escaped.[11]

To declare therefore, as Kautsky did in 1906, that "events have fully justified the Marxian doctrine,"[12] is to misconceive reality to an extraordinary degree. The Bolshevist revolution itself, in spite of appearances, is a refutation of Marx's predictions, for it broke out in the very country of all Europe where capitalist society was the least developed, and where it had least paved the way for communist society. It was an "accident," and it was also a result of the weak political organization of this vast region. The crumbling of the czarist power naturally left the country at the mercy of energetic sectaries. And as a matter of fact capitalism is now arising from its ashes, and really communistic economic organization, maintained by dictatorship, seems on the road to dissolution.

We know that Marx, impressed by the crisis of 1846–1848, counted much on economic crises to evolve a new society. Social revolution cannot break out in periods of prosperity, and it is because the crisis of 1848 was followed by two prosperous years that the counter-revolution carried the day: "Social revolution," Marx declared in 1850, "is possible only in periods in which these two factors, the forces of production and the forms of bourgeois production, come into conflict. A revolution cannot break out until another crisis occurs, but this crisis is as certain to come as the last one." [13]

Economic crises were in fact particularly numerous and serious in the first half of the nineteenth century.[14] However, as Bernstein points out,[15] they became rarer and less formidable in the second half of the century, because of the extension of markets and the development of productivity. It is a significant fact that the crisis of 1900 missed the United States. There may be overproduction in certain industries, and local crises may occur, but they do not necessarily bring about a general crisis. Anarchy in production, which is the cause of crises, has been partially corrected by cartels and trusts, whose efficiency has been exaggerated, however (as Jean Lescure has shown). Bernstein observes that the question cannot be solved *a priori;* general crises might be produced by outside events impossible to foresee, rather than by the play of economic phenomena.[16] In point of fact the economic crises resulting from the world war have strengthened rather than weakened the forces of capitalism. A successful communist revolution has taken place only in Russia, and even there for causes by no means strictly economic.[17] Marxian theorists have finally recognized

82

that it is futile to count on crises to bring about social revolution.[18]

In all civilized countries the socialist parties have come at last to understand that they cannot count on the "catastrophic" revolution. Engels himself admitted that. The resistance of capitalism has been estimated at its real strength. They have ceased to hope for a radical social transformation in the near future, and socialist organizations and labor unions have turned their attention to the daily struggle with capitalistic forces, endeavoring to restrain them as much as possible. Marx himself, who was at first hostile to labor legislation, to factory acts, and even to the organization of labor unions, for fear that partial reforms would attenuate the antagonisms necessary to produce revolution, was obliged to change his opinion. This explains the development of the "reformist" tendency which has been forced upon the socialists of most countries. This fact, much more than the world war, is the deep-seated cause of the recent trend of the Second International.[19] At the same time, as Arthur Wauters [20] points out, the most moderate reformers, such as Mr. and Mrs. Webb, have become increasingly radical, and are coming more and more to consider the reforms as steps on the way to a veritable social revolution.[21] This was the idea of Jaurès, who in his *Etudes socialistes* favored the doctrine of "revolutionary evolution" and sought to discover even in present-day society the germs of the communistic society to come.[22]

Thus if Marx's predictions have not come true, and if the economic evolution of contemporary society has but imperfectly followed the path marked out for it, it is because of the impossibility of formulating the *law* of evolution, that is, a veritable law whose forecasts must inevitably be realized.

Capital, as Bernstein says,[23] is an admirable scientific monument, constructed with great intellectual honesty and instinct with a profound sense of reality; but Marx could never make up his mind to knock down the "scaffolding," which was too small for the structure. He preferred to modify the building. This inconvenient scaffolding is the preconceived doctrine, the product of the dialectic.

It is easy to see how the materialistic conception of history clashed repeatedly with contemporary facts, just as we shall note that it often clashes with historical data. It must be admitted, moreover, that Marx, and still more Engels, who had a less powerful but more elastic mind, profited by experience and abandoned certain parts of their doctrine.

We have seen that Engels finally came to believe that the superstructure is not determined exclusively by the economic foundation. Marx, who at first believed that all reforms would retard the catastrophe that was to set the world free, and so had been opposed to social reforms and the labor union movement, became much less intransigent. The *Communist Manifesto* proclaimed that these legislative reforms affected only the "private interests of the workingman," [24] but in the inaugural address before the International of 1862 Marx declared that the Ten Hour Law was a long step towards social emancipation: "It has not only had great practical effect, but for the first time, in broad daylight, bourgeois political economy has been obliged to strike its colors before the political economy of the workingman." [25]

As it often happens, certain followers showed themselves more uncompromising than their master. One day when Bernstein was endeavoring to show that the number of property holders was increasing, not diminishing, Kautsky replied: "If that were true then the date of our victory would not only be very long postponed, but we should never attain our goal. If it be capitalists who increase and not those with no possessions, then we are going ever further from our goal the more evolution progresses, then capitalism grows stronger, not socialism." [26] Kautsky, following the dialectic conception, considered that progress could arise only from the "aggravation of the situation." [27] Antonio Labriola, for his part, holds more rigorously to the predominance of the "substructure" than Engels or even Marx himself.[28]

PART II

THE MATERIALISTIC CONCEPTION OF HISTORY AND THE PROBLEM OF HISTORICAL KNOWLEDGE

Although in the minds of its founders the materialistic conception of history was essentially intended to lead to practical consequences—economic, social and political—and although they were little concerned with the effect it might have on the abstract and scientific study of history, it is important, nevertheless, to consider the doctrine from the standpoint of historical knowledge. Many historians and economists, without in the least accepting socialism and without taking any part in the political and social discussion, have pronounced themselves in favor of the materialistic conception in the form of an economic interpretation of history.*

It is from this point of view that we will now attempt to criticize the doctrine, the genesis and character of which have been outlined above. Is it true that all historical events, all political and legal institutions, and even all religious and intellectual phenomena are determined solely by economic organization?

---

* See for instance Seligman, op. cit.

CHAPTER VII

POLITICAL AND LEGAL PHENOMENA

IN considering this subject, it will be well first to make a distinction between two categories of phenomena: the accidental, fortuitous facts, on the one hand, and the permanent facts, the institutions, on the other.

It is probable that accidental facts, those which occur only once in the same way, are largely the result of chance and are not determined by general causes. According to the apt definition of Cournot,[1] chance is "the mutual independence of several series of causes and effects, which combine accidentally to produce a certain phenomenon, to bring about a certain encounter, to determine a certain event, which for that reason is called fortuitous." [2]

The effects of chance are obvious everywhere, in history as in nature. In the field of political history, and in particular of political facts, it plays an important part. We may grant this much to Seignobos, even if we cannot entirely agree with him, that the revolutions of 1830 and 1848, which exerted so great an influence on the political evolution of Europe, are to be regarded as pure accidents.[3]

The part played by individuals is also undeniable, especially that played by superior personalities. In a recent work, Kurt Breysig[4] even endeavors to show that it is the creative force of individuals that determines all new movements, while the masses, the collectivity, represent essentially the force of inertia. He shows cleverly that Karl Marx himself, who believed in nothing but the action of the collectivity, contradicted his theory in practice, since no one has demonstrated more clearly, by his own example, the creative force of the individual, no one has contributed so much to awaken class consciousness among the proletariat. The uncompromising partisans of individualism might of course be met with the argument that the most original innovators are largely the product of their time and environment. We might even quote Lavroff to the effect that the individual does not play a great part in the development of humanity unless "he associates himself with the toiling and suffering masses."[5] This very complex question would really seem to be insoluble. All we can say is that however small we consider the rôle of the individual to be, we cannot deny that it exists. It is obvious, moreover, that this rôle increases the number of accidental events of which it is impossible to determine the causes.[6]

As for political institutions themselves, their evolution depends, partially at least, on accidents, such as conquests, or the policy of this or that sovereign or minister. Here it is not so difficult to discover the general tendency of the evolution, but does it depend exclusively on economic phenomena? It does not seem so. Many factors of different kinds come into play, not to mention that, in administrative matters, as Kurt Breysig aptly points out, we often see an internal evolution of the organization, which gradually improves. Thus notwithstanding the weakening of the monarchical idea in France in the eighteenth century, the administration of the royal power improved. History shows that the various ministerial departments, such as the *bureaux des intendances*, gradually increased their own efficiency.[7] That economic facts have exerted an influence, and a very important one, on political institutions and on political evolution in general, would be difficult to deny, but they are not the only factors in question.

It is evident also that political events, such as wars, invasions and conquests, have in many cases contributed largely to modify the economic and in particular the social condition of certain countries. The wars and conquests of republican Rome reduced the number of the middle classes and of the farmers, extended the *latifundia*, and thereby affected the productivity of Italian agriculture.[8]

To come to modern history, was it not the political triumph of the British aristocracy in the eighteenth century which precipitated the enclosure movement—that is, the elimination of peasant ownership for the profit of great holdings? Did not the wars of the sixteenth and seventeenth centuries contribute largely to the development of serfdom in Germany? Was not the final abolition of the seigniorial system in Central Europe due to the revolutions of 1830 and 1848? To destroy seigniorial rights in France the political revolution of 1789 was necessary, a revolution which was itself partially due to economic and social causes.[9]

To cite another typical example, G. Plékhanof, in writing his remarkable *Introduction à l'histoire sociale de la Russie*,[10] adopts the materialistic conception of history without reservation; he accepts it in a way as a dogma.[11] And nevertheless, since he is a conscientious worker, he brings facts to light which flatly contradict this conception. Thus he shows that the victory of the nomads in Little Russia—that is, a political fact—forced the population to fall back towards the north and northwest, which caused the general delay in the civilization of Russia and which finally contributed to the subjection of the peasant classes. The "amassing of Russian lands" by the czars of Moscow also powerfully affected the social and economic evolution of the country, and the same may be said of her struggle with the western powers. It was his foreign policy which compelled Peter the Great to Europeanize his army and administration, the effect of which was to give the nobles full control of their property.[12] Moreover, Plékhanof shows that the agrarian question, and in a general way the geographical environment, have exerted a notable influence on the entire political history of Russia. The German revolution of 1918, by abolishing the political and civil restrictions to which farm laborers were subject, by regulating the length of the working day and by favoring collective bargaining for labor, certainly helped to improve the economic condition of this social class.[13]

Action and reaction of economic and political phenomena: is this not precisely what history reveals, without its being possible always to discover which of the two predominates? Reality is much more complex than Karl Marx imagined.

Between economic and legal phenomena the connection is certainly closer, but is it possible to say that the latter have necessarily been determined by the former? In the first place, all legal rules concerning the family are not exclusively determined by the necessities of production. Religious customs, and in particular the worship of the dead, as Fustel de Coulanges has shown in *The Ancient City*, have powerfully affected legal and even political organization. The constitution of property itself did not have its origin exclusively in economic phenomena.[14] Nowhere is the intermingling of these two categories of facts more marked than in the history of the agrarian question: the property system, which arises not only from economic phenomena, but from political events such as conquest and invasion, reacts in turn on the economic system.

It may even be said that the legal system, conservative by nature and often representing obsolete conditions, tends to retard economic evolution. This idea is familiar to Marx, who considers that the property system represents an outworn form of production. Revolution, in his opinion, results from this loss of balance. We must remember that Marx, as Menger observes,[15] has a tendency to underestimate legal facts, and has therefore not concerned himself with public and social law in the society of which he dreamed.

CHAPTER VIII

RELIGIOUS AND INTELLECTUAL PHENOMENA

ARE religious matters determined by economic phenomena? The attempts of Marx's followers to prove this, invoking the support of historical data, do not seem to have been especially fortunate. Antonia Labriola, for example, has endeavored to show that the history of Christianity can be largely if not entirely explained by the evolution of property and the organization of labor—that is, by the economic life.[1] These phenomena alone, he declares, can explain how a "society of equals," such as existed in primitive Christianity, could become a Church dominated by a strict hierarchy, a State organization, exercising political influence, and a conservative social force. Labriola takes no account of religious beliefs, of faith, or even of political factors.

As a matter of fact the entire history of the Church, which points to the great rôle played by religious beliefs, shows that these views are erroneous, in part, at least. Obviously the fact that Christianity has been forced to compromise with the temporal world has exerted an influence on its destinies. Nor can it be denied that the Holy See, the bishops and the monasteries became very considerable financial powers. For this reason the Church was affected by economic phenomena and contributed in a way to the genesis of a capitalism with which its doctrines conflicted, as shown by its attitude towards the charging of interest on loans, its conception of just price, etc.[2] In this connection the materialistic interpretation seems at least more tenable than the thesis sustained by certain Catholic writers such as Janssen and Cardinal Newman, that the ecclesiastical powers showed themselves more generous and more charitable towards their peasant subjects than did the temporal landlords. Still farther from the truth is the contention of Janssen that the heretical reformers were responsible for the social disturbances of the fifteenth and sixteenth centuries. To refute this we have only to recall Luther's attitude towards the Peasant War of 1525.[3] In those times of intense faith social upheavals naturally took on a religious cast.

We must also be wary of accepting without question the assertion of certain advocates of historical idealism (perhaps we should say "ideologism"), who, in the wake of Max Weber and E. Troeltsch, have claimed to prove that Calvinistic and especially Puritan theology powerfully contributed to the formation of modern capitalism. This theory does contain a grain of truth, however. The formation of the "capitalist mentality," the attribute of the Puritans and of the Jews according to Sombart, would not have much weight in the balance without the immense influence exerted by phenomena of a really economic nature, such as the exploitation of the New World and the consequent influx of precious metals.[4] In short, from this point of view the attempt to beat the materialistic conception of history on its own ground has been unsuccessful.

On the other hand, how can it be maintained that there have never been any but class ethics? Engels himself admits that many thinkers and moralists have risen above these ethics and have professed a really *human* ethical standard. Science and general philosophy, *a fortiori*, escape almost entirely from the influence of economic phenomena; they belong to the domain of the mind.[5]

It must of course be admitted that the development of economic activity has also contributed to intellectual emancipation. This is doubtless the main reason why Italy as early as the fourteenth century and the Netherlands at the dawn of the modern era were the chosen field of science, letters and art, and why the Renaissance was particularly flourishing and fertile in those countries. Taine has brought out this principle very clearly in his *Philosophy of Art*.[6] It is also a significant fact that the intellectual expansion of Holland occurred precisely in the seventeenth century, which also saw the development of her marvelous commercial activity.[7] This is of course not an absolute rule: from 1871 to 1914 unified Germany, so prosperous economically, did not produce any such great writers and philosophers as did the comparatively poor Germany of the eighteenth and first half of the nineteenth centuries. Nor does it seem that the scientific and artistic expansion of the present-day United States, remarkable as it is in many respects, corresponds to the extraordinary economic development. There wholesale production is somewhat overdone; it is the country of uniformity. The diversity of Europe, while doubtless a disadvantage from the point of view of production, seems to be more favorable to intellectual culture. Moreover, the wind bloweth where it listeth: it is not to the economic prosperity of Elizabeth's time that we owe the genius of Shakespeare, nor was it the splendor of Louis XIV's court that gave us men like Molière and Racine.

Furthermore, does not Marx himself implicitly admit that ideas may exert a fairly direct influence on social revolution (although he regards this as inevitable), or at least that it may be hastened by ideas. If he had not thought so he would not have encouraged socialist propaganda, he would not have urged workers to organize, and he would not have hailed with joy the birth of the *International*. This is where ideology, the *Oberbau*, will influence the substructure, the *Unterbau*.[8]

CHAPTER IX

SOCIAL CLASSES, CLASS CONSCIOUSNESS AND CLASS CONFLICT

THE question of social classes, which Karl Marx brought into such prominence,[1] may allow us to get closer to the problem.

Do social classes have their origin, as he stated, in modes of production? It is very doubtful. It has been fairly proved that slavery, as it existed in antiquity, was not in direct correlation with "economy": the master was looking for cheap labor, without much concerning himself with its actual productivity. The question of the legal form of labor passed into the background. In Greece, side by side with slave labor, free labor played an important part.[2] Andler rightly says that the mode of distribution and the mode of production are two very different things, and that the exploitation of man by man is the result of force.[3] At the same time, the passage from slavery to serfdom, and then the emancipation of the serfs, seem to be especially attributable to economic causes.[4] The relations of social facts to economic facts constitute a difficult problem, which can be solved only by numerous scientific investigations.

It does seem probable at least that for a long time social classes were determined by legal rather than economic distinctions, and that in a general way it must always be so. Is it not the castes of India which appear to us as classes par excellence? But modern democracy has abolished legal distinctions, and it may be asked whether economic distinctions, the only ones that subsist, are sufficient to constitute classes properly speaking. Contrary to Marx's belief, capitalism has broken up classes by contributing to the development of individualism, so that it is in the United States, the most capitalistic country in the world, that there is the least distinction between the social classes.[5]

It is true that generally speaking the *proletariat* may be opposed to the *bourgeoisie*, but these two terms are in part abstractions. Capitalism becomes something more and more impersonal and anonymous as speculation, which is its real foundation much more than the process of production, tends to play a predominating rôle. Marx, who at first had been especially concerned with the process, seems finally to have attached more importance to the phenomenon of speculation and gambling. In Book III of *Capital* we read:[6]

"Gain and loss through fluctuations in the price of these titles of ownership, and their centralisation in the hands of railroad kings, etc., naturally becomes more and more a matter of gambling, which takes the place of labor as the original method of acquiring capital and also assumes the place of direct force. This sort of imaginary money wealth does not merely constitute a very considerable part of the money wealth of private people, but also of banking capital, as we have already indicated." [7]

Since many wage earners may hold some of these securities—an infinitesimal block, it is true—the opposition of capital and labor may be disguised. We know what the advocates of social conservatism have made of this fact, and we are acquainted with the sophistry that workers share in capital like the others.[8] This sophism is possible only because the two categories, capitalists and laborers, do not constitute legal classes separated by a clear line of demarcation. However much the two economic classes may be thus partially disguised, the opposition between labor and capital is none the less strong in reality, and the power of capital is none the less formidable.[9]

We can thus understand why *class consciousness*, which does not really show itself until the nineteenth century, and which moreover was greatly favored by industrial concentration, itself a product of capitalist industry, should have awakened at the call of socialist and revolutionary propaganda. O. Festy [10] has clearly shown that in France, under the July monarchy, it was the workers in the small industries in Paris who, won over to the new ideas, were the first to feel this consciousness. In England, where the industrial revolution took place much earlier than in France, the working class awoke much later to the consciousness that it formed a coherent group. There was indeed the Chartist movement, but as early as 1839 the trade unions seem to have fallen away from it, and a militant of the time expressed himself as follows, which speaks volumes on the alleged unity of the working classes: [11]

"Chartism cannot bring about unity among the most poorly paid workers. Men who earn 30 shillings a week do not concern themselves about those who earn 15, and the latter care as little about those who earn 5 or 6. There is an aristocracy among workingmen as well as in the bourgeois world."

This consciousness, which was still so vague in the eighteenth century, emerged very slowly from the domain of the "subconscious." [12] It is true that the formation of the labor International in 1864 did much to give the working class a clearer consciousness and stronger sense of its collective interests, but it was above all the work of the socialist theorists, Karl Marx in particular. Ideology exercised a great influence in this respect, and Kurt Breysig [13] acutely observes that Marx's own action constituted a striking refutation of his materialistic conception of history.

We now arrive at the vexed question of class conflict, which plays a prominent part in Marx's doctrine, as may be seen from the *Communist Manifesto*. Marx believed that class conflicts always existed, and that in them must be sought the key to all political events and in particular revolutions. He even believed that they were necessary to progress.

In so far as the past is concerned, this conclusion seems to be refuted by general history, with which Marx was insufficiently acquainted. Thus at Rome the struggle between patricians and plebeians was not determined solely by economic considerations. Among the plebs there were rich and poor—many more poor than rich, it is true. Doubtless the question of debts and that of land concessions played an important part, but there was a sort of contract between the rich and the poor plebs: the former, desirous of winning honors and gaining access to political power, made an alliance with the latter.[14] "The poor," says Bloch, "placed the weight of their number at the service of ambitions which did not concern them, and thus political and social claims supported each other and marched side by side to victory."

In the religious wars of the sixteenth century each of the two camps contained individuals belonging to very different classes. The English revolutions of the seventeenth century were essentially religious and political, and social questions played a very insignificant part, although for a moment sectaries of very radical opinions, the *levelers* and the *diggers*, held their corner of the stage. In the French Revolution class antagonisms certainly cropped out, but they were on the whole rather vague and incoherent; it was especially the transient question of the food supply that was at issue.[15]

In *Revolution and Counter-Revolution or Germany in 1848*,[16] Marx admits that before 1848 the Austrian bourgeoisie "had never seen working men acting as a class or stand up for their own distinct class interests." In a recent book [17] J. Delevsky endeavors to show how numerous and varied are the antagonisms which do not rest on the divergent economic interests of hostile classes, and that there are conflicts of race, of nationality, etc.[18] He goes still farther and examines all forms of internal antagonism that divide the proletariat: hostility to foreign workmen, hierarchy among workmen of the same country, opposition to female labor, etc. He shows also that in many cases common interests unite employers and workingmen, and even points complacently to the *syndicats jaunes* (that is, "unfair" or "traitor" unions, which serve the employers' interests), although he admits that they are usually inspired by the employers or by reactionary groups. It would doubtless be easy to multiply examples, which would be interesting as showing the complexity of the question.

It is true in a general way, however, that as capitalism displays its power the various fractions of the working class feel themselves more and more of a unit, at least within a given country.[19] In this connection we must not ignore the influence of industrial concentration. Workingmen, grouped in great establishments and crowded in those immense hives that constitute modern industrial centers, necessarily touch elbows much more than workers in scattered industries. The enormous development of means of communication, as well as the action of the press, draw national and international bonds still tighter.

CHAPTER X

REVOLUTION AND THE CATASTROPHE CONCEPTION OF HISTORY

EVERYONE will agree that civil conflicts, clearly characterized, are revolutions. Up to the present, however, history has recorded no revolution which was, properly speaking, a conflict of antagonistic classes. All, even those which have been especially provoked by economic and social causes, have had an essentially political character, and have aimed at the radical transformation, if not the destruction, of the existing political power.

A very striking example is furnished by the French Revolution itself. In the *cahiers* of 1789 all orders of the State unanimously demanded the establishment of a Constitution and administrative reforms. It is true that the Third Estate in a body—that is, the immense majority of the nation—rose against the privileged orders, but the various classes that made up the Third Estate formed a sort of unit or *bloc* to claim equality before the law and in matters of taxation, as well as the abolition of vestiges of the feudal system.

The revolution of July 1830 was also a political

one, and although carried out in fact by the populace of Paris, it was the bourgeoisie that pushed them on to the barricades. In that same year of 1830 the Belgians revolted to dissolve the union with the detested Dutch, although the union secured for them the most valuable economic advantages.[1] Among the September combatants, as Pirenne has shown, the proletariat, the factory workers, were in the minority; the movement was really *national*. It is true that the workers were wretchedly poor, but there was no spirit of revolt among them; they began to move only under the shock of 1830. The Belgian Constitution, which was voted in 1831, placed a property qualification upon the vote without arousing protest. "The social question," says Pirenne, "had not yet arisen and class spirit was not yet born; the political question was the only one taken into consideration."

Albert Crémieux shows in his excellent thesis [2] that the revolution of 1848 was not only a popular revolution but a national one "in which bourgeoisie and workingmen launched a common attack against conservative royalty." The national guard, composed of bourgeois elements, fought vigorously. While the serious economic crisis of 1846–1847 was doubtless the deep-seated cause of the movement, socialist and democratic agitation also had something to do with it. There was profound and general discontent.

REVOLUTION AND THE CATASTROPHE

The Russian revolution of 1917 is still too recent for history to be able to arrive at an accurate estimate of it. It seems, however, that the first wave was a spontaneous movement of the entire nation against czarism; as to the Bolshevist revolution, it appears to have been a sudden manœuvre by a minority desirous of seizing the power and establishing the dictatorship of the proletariat.

Karl Marx himself, in *Revolution and Counter-Revolution or Germany in 1848*, shows that in Germany, and still more so in Austria, all classes except the feudal aristocracy and the military and civilian officers rose against the governments. He adds: [3]

"But it is the fate of all revolutions that this union of different classes, *which in some degree is always the necessary condition of any revolution*, cannot subsist long. No sooner is the victory gained against the common enemy than the victors become divided among themselves into different camps, and turn their weapons against each other. It is this rapid and passionate development of class antagonism which, in old and complicated social organisms, makes a revolution such a powerful agent of social and political progress; it is this incessantly quick upshooting of new parties succeeding each other in power, which, during those violent commotions, makes a nation pass in five years over more ground than it would have done in a century under ordinary circumstances."

In many respects this is a profound reflection, and might be made the subject of prolonged discussion.

It is also a striking fact that the French Revolution, the only one which had distinctly social results, changed the legal system of the country rather than the economic. Seigniorial rights were abolished and the sale of national property increased. The conditions of peasant property were ameliorated to a marked degree, thus precipitating the previous course of evolution; but agricultural processes and exploitation remained precisely what they had been under the old regime. Neither was industrial organization transformed. These legal modifications finally affected the economic conditions of France, but only indirectly. In its immediate consequences as well as in its character, the French Revolution was of vast importance from the legal and political point of view, but not from the economic.[4]

It is particularly worthy of note that from the conception of class conflict Karl Marx derives his thesis of the sudden passage from a given social system to the opposite system, that is of the *catastrophic* revolution. This conception seems to be absolutely contrary to the realities of history, since transformations ordinarily come about gradually. Even after a radical revolution, there remain many traces of the old regime, and by certain details the future system announces its arrival a long time beforehand. Thus if we consider the industrial revolution in England in the eighteenth and nineteenth centuries, we see that the small industries, small trades and businesses, have not yet disappeared, although the system of large scale industries had in general carried the day. On the other hand, capitalist industries began to make their appearance as early as the sixteenth and seventeenth centuries.[5] It is to be noted that the catastrophic conception derives very directly from the Hegelian dialectic, from the fusion of contradictory propositions. No wonder it clashes with reality.

Marx absolutely neglected, moreover, to investigate the relations which may exist between evolution and revolutions. Do revolutions suddenly interrupt evolution, or, on the contrary, hasten it? What new element do they bring in? This is a very complicated question, of which we can only state the terms here.

Karl Marx, believing in abrupt transformations, is naturally disposed to cut history up into clearly defined periods: thus in *Capital* he continually refers to the pre-capitalistic period. As a matter of fact this *periodisierung*, as the Germans call it, interests philosphers more than it does historians. The latter, thanks to their constant dealing with concrete facts, better understand the complexity of events and institutions and the more subtle distinctions. It is a striking fact that a writer like Troeltsch, who theoretically considers *periodisierung* as one of the essential tasks of the philosophy of history, in practice finds it very difficult to establish clear-cut historical periods, even when he considers the European world alone (*Europäismus*, in which he includes the American continent), and his difficulty increases as he approaches modern times.[6]

CHAPTER XI

TO WHAT EXTENT IS THE ECONOMIC INTERPRETATION VALID?

IN spite of the criticisms that may be directed against the materialistic conception of history, it must be admitted that it contains a large element of truth. Furthermore, it has effectively stimulated investigations in economic history.

For the last half century in fact, many historians have pronounced in favor of the economic interpretation of history without in any way accepting the social doctrine of Marxism,[1] beginning with Thorold Rogers, who does not refer to the work of Karl Marx. He does not believe that economic phenomena form the foundation of history, but he considers that they have an extremely important influence. "I am convinced," he says,[2] "that to omit or neglect these economical facts is to make the study of history barren, and its annals unreal."[3] He is, however, an enterprising investigator rather than a powerful thinker. At the end of the last century Sir William Ashley, the eminent historian, endeavored to show the importance of economic history, but he did not believe that economic phenomena determined all other manifestations of human activity.[4]

In the second third of the nineteenth century a large number of historians, particularly in Germany, abandoned political history, the history of nations, as Ranke conceived it, to investigate the collective facts —civilization, in short—and to give economic phenomena the first place. These new tendencies are brilliantly illustrated by such scholars as Kurt Breysig,[5] Eberhard Gothein,[6] and especially K. Lamprecht, who, between 1891 and 1895, published six volumes of his *Deutsche Geschichte*. Finally, it must be remembered that the great French historian Fustel de Coulanges, in his *Institutions de l'ancienne France*, examined in particular the economic and social facts. For the last thirty years, moreover, investigations in economic history have multiplied in all countries.[7]

It is certain that the economic interpretationist is in a more advantageous position, from the scientific point of view, than the marxist, because, though imbued with political and social ideas, he is as a scholar free from any preoccupation with them. But on the other hand, if he is more economist than historian, there is still considerable danger of his not being truly judicial. The fact is that economics has for a long time busied itself with practical applications, and has

114

been more interested in politics than in science. The liberal orthodox economists are no less to be criticised on this point and no more to be distrusted than the disciples of Marx. Moreover even the wholly disinterested economist tends to consider economic phenomena somewhat *in abstracto*, if he has not had a rigorous historical or philosophical education.

However that may be the economic interpretation of history is on solid ground. There is no doubt that economic phenomena exert considerable influence on the progress of history. How can we really understand the organization of any society if we do not know the organization of labor, the system of industry, the commercial customs, the agrarian regime, etc.? This is true of all epochs. The wars of Louis XIV's reign, which used to be attributed solely to dynastic intrigues, were primarily due to the commercial rivalry of the principal nations of Europe.[8] The great oversea discoveries and the seizure of the New World by the various maritime Powers of Europe have exercised an enormous influence on world history since the sixteenth century. Examples might be multiplied indefinitely.

If it is too much to claim that religious phenomena have been determined by economic causes, it is certain that they have in many cases been influenced by the geographical environment and the social organization. Sylvain Lévi [9] thus explains the persistence of Brahminism in India. A few handfuls of Aryans brought their higher civilization to India and found an immense country inhabited by black races in a state of semi-savagery, and they had to contend with Nature in the formidable aspect she assumes in the tropics. It was Brahminism, with its rigid caste system, which enabled them to maintain their civilization: "Brahminism was one with the social order and was merged with it." This is moreover a remarkable example of the convergence of phenomena of various kinds.

It is also the economic factor which to a certain extent explains the different destinies of humanism and the Reformation in the sixteenth century. In the first third of the century the two movements marched side by side, and there was a close union of forces against the inertia of the middle ages. About 1535, however, divergences began to appear, which became more and more accentuated. It is true they were for the most part due to intellectual causes: for the reformers, free criticism stopped short of the Bible, and for humanists it stopped nowhere. Furthermore, the new aspect which the Reformation took on with Calvin alienated the most liberal spirits, like Rabelais.[10] If, however, humanism failed for the time being, it was only because it was a purely intellectual force. The Reformation, on the contrary, had solid temporal support, both political and material. Lutheranism triumphed chiefly because it was supported in Germany and Sweden by princes desirous of reinforcing their temporal power with the spiritual power it would confer upon them and by the secularization of church property.[11] The success of Anglicanism can be similarly explained, and Calvinism mixed more and more with the material world until its original doctrine became adulterated. Time was working for humanism, however, which represented something purer. It was to have its revenge later.

It is also to be noted that economic phenomena are less subject than others to disturbances caused by "accidents" (that is, by "chance" or unpredictable events), or by the influence of powerful individualities. To a certain degree economic phenomena fall into the domain of statistics, and while they may not be subject to *laws* properly so-called, we can at least note certain tendencies in their evolution.[12] History is more at ease with them than with political facts, which are much less regular and more subject to the effects of chance. They are therefore a more solid substance for historical investigation than other phenomena.[13]

It is true that the great difficulty is always to make a *quantitative* estimate of the respective importance of economic facts and others. This importance varies according to time and place. We may recall in this connection the judicious observations of Eduard Bernstein. Since we pay more attention now to economic factors, he says, we are inclined to believe that they are more important today than they used to be. In reality it is rather the reverse: science, art and most social relations depend less rigidly upon the type of economy than formerly. As the economic field opens out, Bernstein concludes, determinism becomes feebler and independence stronger.[14] In these matters we have only indications, precise measurement being impossible in the present state of our knowledge. Very likely it always will be,[15] since phenomena of various sorts are so intermingled that it is very difficult to distinguish cause and effect.[16] The important thing is to have stated the problem. Let us be grateful to Marx and Engels for having first brought it out into broad daylight.

CHAPTER XII

CONCLUSION

IT is not difficult to see why the attempt of Karl Marx was doomed to partial failure. It showed great power of mind but it had the prime defect of not being a disinterested scientific product. The *Communist Manifesto* is convincing proof that its founder saw in it a weapon of political and social warfare.[1] Furthermore, and this is doubtless its main defect, it rests less on the study of facts than on an *a priori* conception, which Marx and Engels tried later to confirm by observing past and present facts, not altogether without twisting these facts to suit their ideas. In reality the Marxian doctrine, especially in the beginning, invoked history less than philosophy, and tended to confuse the two fields.

We must remember that Hegel was at first Marx's master, and that the pupil remained faithful to the dialectic method of his teacher. It is true that he claims to have done just the reverse, and not entirely without reason, since in place of making reality depend upon thought, as Hegel attempted to do, Marx considered the material world as the foundation of all ideology. At bottom, however, it is the same process, for like Hegel he attempted to explain everything as deriving from a single source. To this extent he may be considered, if not an idealist, at least an "ideologist." For this reason, in spite of his acute sense of concrete facts about the past, and especially in the present, he often comes into conflict with reality, which is so infinitely complex and in which such diverse phenomena are intermingled. Even his profound and scientific study, *Capital*, proceeds from a largely metaphysical hypothesis. It will be understood therefore why his materialistic conception of history, and in particular his thesis of class struggle, is more logical when considered abstractly, apart from exceptions and contingencies, than when examined in the light of concrete facts.

Marx was quite sincere in the conviction that his doctrine was really scientific, in the fullest sense of the word. He believed that it could not only explain economic and social facts, but also determine *laws* capable of foretelling the future. "Critical communism," declares Labriola,[2] "foresees the future because what it says and predicts must inevitably happen by the immanent necessity of history, seen and studied henceforth in the foundation of its economic substructure." Engels himself declared that the law of historical materialism discovered by Marx was comparable in importance to the law of gravitation discovered by Newton. He mistook for a law what is only a theory; in history, there is no law capable of rigidly forecasting the future.

Marx firmly believed in the laws of historical evolution precisely because he considered only one category of antecedents: "The hand mill," he says in the *Poverty of Philosophy*,[3] "will produce a society with a feudal lord as surely as the steam mill will produce a society with the industrial capitalist."

We read moreover in *Capital*:[4] "Factory legislation, that first conscious and methodical reaction of society against the spontaneously developed form of the process of production is, as we have seen, just as much the necessary product of modern industry as cotton yarn, self-actors, and the electric telegraph."

Andler strongly reproaches Marx for this determinism,[5] on the ground that it cannot be established by history, which does not observe its facts at first hand: "There is no science more *ideological* than history, because *of all sciences it is the only one which never deals with reality*." This is not convincing because history, though obliged to comprehend the facts of the past indirectly, by the traces left behind, nevertheless aspires to *reality*. We know that even the exact sciences try to subject reality to reason, that they are thus in a sense as ideological as the social sciences, and that they even contain an element of metaphysics.[6] Furthermore, determinism is impossible in history because the facts are too complicated and because the "accidents," the fortuitous events, are so numerous that it would be impossible to determine the laws of evolution. There is nothing more dangerous than to liken history to the physical sciences, and to try to formulate *historical laws* analogous to those which these scientists have been able to establish.[7]

The great defect of the materialistic conception of history is that it is one sided, that is sees only one aspect of things, since it depreciates legal and intellectual phenomena. On the other hand, historical idealism, or rather "ideologism," also sees but one side, and that a much more restricted one. We know, for instance, that a whole category of historians, consciously or unconsciously inspired by partisan spirit, are endeavoring to prove that the French Revolution of 1789 was the work of intellectual societies, of freemasonry.[8] They deliberately ignore the innumerable phenomena, the profound or direct causes which lay back of the upheaval.[9] As a matter of fact, even the powerful intellectual movement of the eighteenth century cannot be considered as the real cause of the revolutionary crisis. The spread of philosophic ideas doubtless contributed to prepare the public mind to desire a radical change in the entire political and social system; but other forces came into play, among them the economic interests of the social classes which suffered from the old regime. It is true that once the revolutionary movement was started the political, economic and social doctrines of the eighteenth century helped to give it a certain orientation.[10] On the whole, however, we may conclude that the intellectual and political angle gives a still more restricted historical view of things than the materialistic conception.[11]

Let us admit then that this doctrine, as conceived by its founders,[12] who were moreover less uncompromising and broader-minded than some of their over-zealous followers, appears as a powerful structure which contains solid materials and a notable element of truth. The materialistic conception and economic interpretation of history have rendered and still render noteworthy services. Their outstanding merit has been to free us from the idea that great men make history, and to draw the attention of historians to the less dramatic phenomena which reveal economic life and that "silent" mass of workers, as Unamuno describes them, who are without doubt the real actors in the human drama.[13] Furthermore in the infinite sea of historical events, economic determinism has helped to furnish us with a guiding thread which keeps us from being lost. It has resurrected the notion of the *universal*, which, somewhat obfuscated by erudition—by indispensable erudition—was in danger of becoming lost to view. From this standpoint its philosophical import has been considerable. While it may be far from fulfilling all the requirements of historical criticism, and often clashes with historical data precisely because its founders believed too firmly in the existence of historical or economic laws, it has at least contributed to a better understanding of both the past and the present, and to a more scientific attitude toward history.

NOTES

CHAPTER I

[1] Ludwig Woltmann: *Der historische Materialismus*, Düsseldorf, 1900. This work has been a very valuable aid in studying the doctrine. See also the excellent works of Edwin R. A. Seligman: *The Economic Interpretation of History*, New York, 1902, and of C. Barbagallo: *Che cosa è il materilismo storica*, Milan, 1925 (extracts published in the *Nuova Rivista Storica*, vol. VIII and IX).

[2] For the following remarks see in particular E. R. A. Seligman, op. cit., and the valuable collection *Aus dem literarischen Nachlass von Karl Marx, Friedrich Engels, und F. Lassalle*, F. Mehring, Stuttgart, Vol. I.

[3] L. Woltmann, op. cit., pp. 142–143.

[4] For the entire communist and socialistic movement of 1840–1848, see Charles Andler: *Introduction au Manifeste communiste*, Paris, 1901.

[5] "Das Verhältnis der Industrie, überhaupt der Welt des Reichthums zur der politischen Welt ist ein Hauptproblem der modernen Zeit" (*Deutsch-französische Jahrbücher*, Nos. 1 and 2, 1844, p. 75). See L. Woltmann, op. cit., pp. 143 ff.

[6] *Aus dem literarischen Nachlass*, vol. I, pp. 384 ff. In English in *Selected Essays*, New York, 1926 (International Publishers).

[7] French translation by L. Rémy, Paris, Schleicher, 1899. Various English editions, e.g., Chicago, Charles H. Kerr, 1907.

[8] See also *Die Heilige Familie*, a pamphlet directed by Marx

and Engels against the Young Hegelian Bruno Bauer (*Aus dem literarischen Nachlass*, vol. II).

[The expression "Social lag" is sometimes used in America to convey Marx's point that technological evolution tends to outrun social change. *Translator*.]

[9] Marx's "On Feuerbach" is found in English as an appendix to the translation of Engels' *Feuerbach, the Roots of Socialist Philosophy*, Chicago, 1908.

[10] "Seine sinnlichen Beziehungen, noch nicht gesellschaftlich und historisch gefasst." See L. Woltmann, op. cit., pp. 157 ff.

[11] The Stuttgart (German) edition is the one followed here.

[12] Charles Andler says that Engels had certainly been inspired by Eugène Buret's work: *La misère de la classe ouvrière en France et Angleterre*, 2 vol., 1840. This is doubtless true, but Engels' work is much more accurate and more logically thought out.

[13] Some of these ideas are expressed by Engels as early as 1843 in his *Umrisse zu einer Kritik der Nationaloekonomie* (*Aus dem literarischen Nachlass*, vol. I, pp. 432–460). According to Rodolfo Mondolfo (*Le matérialisme historique d'aprés Frédéric Engels*), Engels, who was more of an economist than a philosopher, gave substance to a conception which Marx, who had at first been given over to philosophic speculation, had already worked out. In any case the two men worked in close collaboration from 1845 on.

[14] Mondolfo thinks that the word "materialism" is unfortunate. The Marxian conception is rather a *realistic* conception, as opposed to Hegel's *idealistic* conception. Marx reasons not from the idea but from concrete human needs.

[15] On Utopian socialism see F. Engels: *Herrn Eugen Dühring's Umwälzung der Wissenschaft*, 1878, 3rd edition, 1894, pp. 274 ff. In English edition, *Landmarks of Scientific*

NOTES

Socialism translated by Austin Lewis, Chicago, 1907, pp. 236 ff.

[16] See also his articles in the *Westfälischer Dampfboot*.

[17] *Introduction au Manifeste communiste*, pp. 71 ff.

[18] G. von Below (*Comienzo y objectivo de la sociologia*, in the *Anuario de historia del derecho espanol*, vol. III, 1926) states that, earlier than Marx, Lorenz von Stein, in his *Socialisme et le communisme de la France contemporaine* 1842–50), had emphasized the influence of economic facts, and that as early as 1837 J. W. von Raumer had given a real economic interpretation of history. In the first half of the nineteenth century some Argentine historians had a similar idea; Alberdi in particular contends that the Argentine revolution of 1810 was essentially due to the desire and necessity for economic emancipation. See Ricardo Lavene: *Interpretacion economica de la historia argentina* (*Anuario de historia del derecho espanol*, vol. III, 1926). But this is rather the economic interpretation of history than the materialistic conception proper.

[19] A synthesis which not only represents the total of the elements composing it, but which gives more than all those elements put together.

[20] The French version of C. Andler (Paris, 1901) is followed in the original. There are numerous English editions. The one used as a check is Samuel Moore's translation of 1888, revised by Engels; published by Charles H. Kerr and Company, Chicago, 1912.—Translator.

[21] *Essays on the Materialistic Conception of History*, translated by Charles H. Kerr, Chicago, 1908, pp. 16 ff.

[22] The *Communist Manifesto* may be compared with Karl Marx's speech before the Cologne jury in 1849. He declared that the revolution of 1789 was not a "political conflict, but a social conflict that took on a political form"; a bureaucratic-feudal society was in conflict with a modern bourgeois society: a society of free competition with that of the trade guilds; a

society of landed property with that of industry; a society of faith with that of science.

CHAPTER II

[1] Op. cit., p. 108. See also K. Marx: *Le 18 brumaire de Louis Bonaparte*, preface of 1869: "I am showing that the class conflict in France has created circumstances and situations such that it has been possible for a mediocre and grotesque personage to play an historic rôle." English version, *The Eighteenth Brumaire of Louis Bonaparte*, translated by Daniel de Leon, Chicago, 1914.

[2] From the French translation of 1900.

[3] Op. cit., p. 244.

[4] See Engels' letter of September 21, 1890 (*Sozialistische Akademiker*, 1895, p. 351), quoted also by Woltmann, op. cit., pp. 249–250, and by A. Labriola, *Socialisme et philosophie*, French translation, pp. 239 ff.: "Nach materialistischer Geschichtsauffassung ist das in letzter Instanz bestimmende Moment in der Geschichte, die Produktion und Reproduktion des wirklichen Lebens. *Mehr hat Marx noch ich je behauptet.* Wenn nun jemand dahin verdreht, das oekonomische Moment sei das einzig bestimmende, so verwandelt er jenen Satz in eine nichtssagende, abstrakte, absurde Phrase. Die oekonomische Lage ist die Basis, aber die verschiedenen Momente des Oberbaues—politische Formen des Klassenkampfes und seine Resultate—Verfassungen, nach gewonnener Schlacht durch die siegende Klasse festgestellt, u.s.w. Rechtsformen und nun gar die Reflexe aller dieser wirklichen Kämpfe in Gehirn der Beteiligten, politische, jurische, philosophische Theorien, religiöse Anschauungen auch deren Weiterentwicklung zu Dogmensystemen, üben auch ihre Einwirkung auf den Verlauf der

NOTES

geschichtlichen Kämpfe aus und bestimmen in vielen Fällen vorwiegend deren Form." In this same letter Engels states that it would be absurd to attribute the rôle of the Prussian state to economic causes alone.

[5] This is also the interpretation given by P. Barth in *Die Geschichts-philosophie Hegel's und der Hegelianer bis auf Marx und Hartmann*, Leipzig, 1890, pp. 40 ff.

[6] A. Labriola: *Socialisme et philosophie*, pp. 246 ff. and 256 ff. R. Mondolfo, op. cit., pp. 351 ff., believes that Marx and Engels, in spite of apparent contradictions, never had any other conception, and that for them economic phenomena are of first importance, although political, legal and religious phenomena and even philosophical doctrines themselves react in their turn on economic phenomena. Mondolfo cites interesting documents in this connection, but the thought of Marx and Engels is not very clear, especially since they never gave any general explanation of their doctrine of historical materialism. See also Charles Turgeon: *La conception matérialiste de l'histoire* (Travaux juridiques et économiques de l'Université de Rennes, vol. III, 1911.).

[7] This conception is very questionable. Many scientific discoveries seem to be the fruit of absolutely disinterested research; and Engels takes no account of the delight in research and speculation which impels the scholar and the philosopher. The arguments he advances to prove the indirect influence of the economic condition on philosophic doctrine are unconvincing, and amount to pure sophistry. Practical inventions are, of course, a different matter.

CHAPTER III

[1] See Henri Sée: *Science et philosophie de l'histoire*, Paris, 1927, Part I, Ch. VII.

[2] It must be noted, however, that in 1849 Marx published articles on wages and capital, in which he studied the passage from slavery to serfdom, then from serfdom to wage earning, and endeavored to prove that these legal transformations were determined by changes in economic life, especially in the mode of production.

[3] English translation by E. M. Aveling, London, 1896.

[4] The ideas developed in *Revolution and Counter-Revolution* had already been set forth by Marx in his articles in the *Neue Rheinische Zeitung* in 1850 (*Aus dem literarischen Nachlass*, vol. III, pp. 87 ff.).

[5] But he does entirely misinterpret the meaning of the Slavic nationalist movements. See also his 1850 work: *Der demokratische Panslavismus* (*Aus dem literarischen Nachlass*, vol. III, pp. 246 ff.): "War to the death on Slavism, which is a traitor to the revolution; a war of extermination and merciless terrorism against it, not in the interest of Germany, but in that of the revolution." He believed that without Russia the Slav movements would not exist.

[6] *Der deutsche Bauernkrieg*, 1850, Leipzig edition, 1875.

[7] The first volume of *Capital* was issued in 1867.

[8] The rather feeble English rendering of this is found in *Capital*, vol. I, Ch. XXVI, p. 786, Moore and Aveling translation, Charles H. Kerr and Company, Chicago, 1921. Translator.

[9] See R. H. Tawney: *Religion and the Rise of Capitalism*, London, 1926, and *The Agrarian Problem in the Sixteenth Century*, 1912.

[10] *Capital*, vol. I, Chs. XXIX and XXX.

[11] Op. cit. Ch. XXXI.

[12] Ibid. p. 833.

[13] See for example E. R. A. Seligman and V. G. Simkhovitch, op. cit.; also K. Kautsky: *Le marxisme et son critique*

Bernstein, translation, Leray-Martin, Paris, 1900, p. 15. German edition, *Bernstein und das Socialdemokratische Programm; eine Antikritik*, Stuttgart, 1899.

CHAPTER IV

[1] *Essays on the Materialistic Conception of History*, p. 126,

[2] See Woltmann, op. cit. Also the excellent work of Victor Basch: *Les doctrines politiques des philosophes classiques de l'Allemagne*, Paris, 1927.

[3] E. Meyerson: *De l'explication dans les sciences*, vol. II, pp. 35 ff.

[4] E. Troeltsch: *Der Historismus und seine Probleme*, Tübingen, 1922, pp. 243 ff.

[5] Kurt Breysig endeavors, it is true, to show that Hegel does not apply his dialectic method to history (*Vom geschichtlichen Werden*, vol. II, pp. 134 ff.), but that would not prevent Marx from so employing this general method.

[6] Op. cit., pp. 314 ff.

[7] See also Kurt Breysig: op. cit., vol. II, pp. 84 ff.

[8] Italics ours.

[9] *The Poverty of Philosophy*, the Twentieth Century Press Ltd., London, 1900, p. 91. See also pp. 127 ff. on competition and monopoly.

[10] On the virtues of dialectic in the view of Marx and Engels, see also the latter's Anti-Dühring, 3rd German edition, pp. 137–146: "the negation of negation," he says, "is a process current in everyday life and in all science; this law was formulated, and only formulated, by Hegel, and for the first time with the maximum precision." "What all these gentlemen lack," he says in another place, "is dialectic; for them Hegel never existed" (letter of October 27, 1890, published

by A. Labriola, *Socialisme et philosophie*, p. 257). The English version of this work of Engels is published under the title of *Landmarks of Scientific Socialism*, Charles H. Kerr and Company, Chicago, 1907. For a discussion of the dialectic, see Ch. VII, in particular, the section on "Negation of the Negation," pp. 159 ff.

[11] R. Mondolfo, op. cit., pp. 60 ff., also believes that the "scientific socialism" of Marx is directly derived from Hegelian logic, but he is far from considering that this weakens the Marxian doctrine.

[12] *Die Voraussetzungen des Sozialismus und die Aufgaben der Sozialdemokratie*, Stuttgart, 1899, pp. 27 ff. English title, *Evolutionary Socialism; a Criticism and an Affirmation*, London and New York, 1909, Ch. I, passim.

[13] It may be very freely translated: To seek after truth by the light of dialectic is like trying to light up the dark with a will-o'-the-wisp. Mondolfo, op. cit., pp. 347 ff., considers that the contradiction noted by Bernstein does not exist in reality; his argument seems more subtle than convincing.

[14] See in this connection the interesting remarks of Henri de Man, *Au-delà du marxisme*, Brussels, 1927, pp. 277 ff.

[15] On the criticism of constructive political economy see F. Simiand, *La méthode positive en science économique*, Paris, 1912.

[16] See Henri Sée: *Science et philosophie de l'histoire*, Paris, 1927, Part I, Ch. VII.

[17] See Léopold Leseine: *L'influence de Hegel sur Marx*, Paris, 1907 (law thesis). He says that Marx is made up of two men: Dr. Marx, the scholar in his study, and Citizen Marx, the man of action, tribune and pamphleteer. See also G. H. Bousquet: *Essai sur l'évolution de la pensée économique*, Paris, 1927.

[18] He reproaches Proudhon (*Misère de la philosophie*, French

translation, p. 177) with making out of certain economic phenomena such as the division of labor "eternal laws and simple and abstract categories, instead of considering the evolution of phenomena." Compare this literal translation from the French version, with the English edition previously cited, pp. 107 ff.

[19] *Historical Materialism and the Economics of Karl Marx*, New York, 1914, p. 18 ff.

[20] See the critical review of *Past and Present* by Friedrich Engels, *Lage Englands*, in *Aus dem literarischen Nachlass*, vol. I, pp. 481 ff.

CHAPTER V

[1] Op. cit., pp. 255 ff. See also H. Greulich: *Ueber die materialistische Geschichtsauffassung*, Berlin, 1897.

[2] Any socialist theorist might be characterized to some extent in the same way. This does not mean that a socialist cannot pursue the scientific method in his writings, nor that he is excluded from making full use, in support of his doctrine, of the usual economic arguments. Yet the moment that he is preoccupied mainly with the practical applications of economics he ceases to be a *scientist*, in the strict sense of the word. In this respect we might contrast the physiocrats, the economists of the so-called liberal school and the socialists. Only in the quite contemporary period has it been clearly understood that political economy should be as objective and disinterested as language or any "social science." See René Gonnard: *Histoire des doctrines économiques*, vol. III, Paris, 1922, and especially G. H. Bousquet, op. cit. It is even conceivable that an economist might have socialistic convictions—or even more radical collectivist opinions—and at the same time criticize,

as a scholar, in part or as a whole, the Marxian doctrine. In socialism, there is a question of faith, almost of religion. Therein, it would seem, lies its greatness.

[3] *The Poverty of Philosophy* and *Aus dem literarischen Nachlass*, vol. II, p. 416.

[4] See for example the recollections of Paul Lafargue, W. Liebknecht and F. Lessner in D. Riazonov's *Karl Marx, homme, penseur et révolutionnaire*, Paris, 1928.

[5] Ibid., Preface, p. 7.

[6] Vol. I, Ch. XXXI.

[7] Compare Jean Jaures: *Idéalism et matérialisme dans la conception de l'histoire*, Lille, 1901, p. 20: "Did Marx himself not bring back into his conception of history the notion of the ideal, of progress, of right? He not only proclaims communistic society as the necessary consequence of the capitalistic order, but shows that such a society will see the end of that class antagonism which is exhausting humanity."

[8] See in this connection the very judicious observations of Woltmann, op. cit., pp. 206 ff., and Mondolfo, op. cit., pp. 388 ff. Marx does not adopt the ethical point of view, but an ethical system emerges from his conception.

[9] We should add that the theory of *surplus value* implicitly contains a conception of justice, the idea of a man's right to the entire product of his labor. It is true that Marx did not explicitly draw this conclusion from it, but the congresses of the *International* and the Gotha program deduced it, and it is this conception that has so powerfully contributed to the spread of Marxism and to its power of persuasion. See A. Menger: *Le droit au produit intégral du travail*, French translation, 1900, pp. 137 ff., and the Introduction of Andler, op. cit., pp. xxxiv ff. See also B. Croce, op. cit. pp. 48 ff., and Leseine, op. cit.

[10] L. Woltmann, op. cit., p. 375.

[11] On the rôle which they attribute to the will see Mondolfo, op. cit., Ch. IX.

[12] Bourguin justly remarks (op. cit., p. 342): "Perhaps it was necessary to make promises as vast as the total expropriation of the capitalists and the dawn of an era of universal happiness in order to arouse the masses, to awake their enthusiasm and to spread the faith that leads to blind devotion."

[18] Jaurès also is thinking of the interests of socialist propaganda when he states that the Marxian doctrine must be adopted practically without restriction. See his lecture on *Bernstein et l'évolution de la méthode socialiste*, Paris, 1926, in which he does not squarely face the difficulties. When Jaurès speaks as an historian—and he has shown an admirable historical sense in his *Histoire de la Révolution*—he is not afraid to declare that the materialistic conception of history does not furnish an exhaustive explanation of historical reality. His broad-mindedness is in happy contrast with the narrowness of the uncompromising marxists. In *La Constituante*, 1st edition, pp. 755–756 he says: "The conception of economic determinism which explains great events by the class relationships, is an excellent guide through the complication and confusion of the facts, but it does not go to the bottom of historical reality. To begin with, it is hardly necessary to say that it does not furnish the key to individual differences. Why, for example, was Robespierre the fanatical theorist of democracy, and Barnave the brilliant apologist of the bourgeoisie?

"There is scarcely a human individual who ceases entirely to be a man in order to become solely the member of a social class. Thus in innumerable minds—in innumerable centers of energy—an almost indefinable basis of humanity composed of age-old traditions and confused aspirations is blended to produce the determined action of immediate interests. Furthermore, the classes themselves as such have something more than class consciousness, just as the same chemical elements form very different combinations at different temperatures. There is such a thing as a "moral temperature," a human temperature, which forms very diverse historical combinations from the same economic elements.

"The ardent education propagated by Rousseau, followed by the drama of the Revolution itself, so raised the moral temperature that the combination of democracy and humanity was realized, and the evolution of economic relationships alone remained to be stimulated a century later."

CHAPTER VI

[1] Op. cit., pp. 40 ff. See also V. G. Simkhovitch: *Marxism versus Socialism*, New York, 1913, pp. 46 ff.

[2] Kautsky, op. cit., pp. 153 ff., remarks not unjustly that the statistics used by Bernstein are difficult to interpret, and that England is in an exceptional position, since she draws her capital from the whole world. In England, moreover, it is a question more particularly of commercial and financial capital, and as to the shares, it is difficult to determine who holds them (pp. 187 ff.).

[3] On the criticism of the Marxian conception, see also Bourguin's discerning treatise: *Les systèmes socialistes et l'évolution économique*, Paris, 1904.

[4] "The revolutionary force," he says, in the work already cited (p. 80), "is not, from the Marxian point of view, capital in general, but industrial capital; this constitutes the force which creates the conditions for the development of capitalist production and which gives birth to the proletariat. On the other hand, commercial capital and loan capital do not constitute revolutionary forces, nor do they create a revolutionary

proletariat." It seems, on the contrary, that industrial capitalism is today more and more subordinated to financial capitalism. See the pertinent remarks of Arturo Labriola: *Il capitalismo*, Naples, 1926, pp. 275 ff.

[5] See P. Caboue: *La concentration des capitaux en France de 1914 à 1919*, in the *Revue d'économie politique*, July, 1920; Arthur Wauter: *L'evolution du marxisme*, Brussels, 1924, pp. 38 ff. In France, this concentration is less rapid than in England.

[6] *Capital*, vol. III, Ch. XLVII, p. 938, Untermann translation from the 1st German edition, Chicago, 1909.

[7] *Op. cit.*, p. 938.

[8] Kautsky recognizes this fact himself (op. cit., pp. 132 ff.), but considers that "the rural population will have less and less influence on social evolution as a whole."

[9] Marx's own expression in *Revolution and Counter-revolution or Germany in 1848*, p. 43.

[10] See Zagorsky: *La République des Soviets*, 1922; Daudé-Bancel: *La crise du régime agraire en Russie*, Paris, 1926.

[11] See Auge-Laribé: *L'évolution argicole de la France*, 1912.

[12] Preface to the *Communist Manifesto*, German edition, 1906.

[13] *Aus dem literarischen Nachlass*, vol. III, p. 467.

[14] The crisis of 1847–48 was especially serious in France and England.

[15] Compare with the English translation already cited, pp. 75 ff.; also with V. G. Simkhovitch, op. cit.

[16] In regard to crises, see also Bourguin, op. cit., pp. 311 ff.; Ansiaux: *Traité d'Economie politique*, vol. III, Paris, 1926, pp. 288 ff.; and in particular Jean Lescure: *Des crises générales et périodiques de surproduction*, Bordeaux, 1906 (law thesis), 3rd edition, Paris, 1926.

[17] On the other hand, Marx was clear-sighted when he proved that the great cause of economic disturbance is that the capacity of production exceeds the purchasing capacity of the workers.

[18] See Tugan-Baranowski: *Studien zur Theorie und Geschichte Handelskrisen in England*, Jena, 1910. Compare Jean Lescure, op. cit.

[19] Contrary to the belief of Paul-Louis: *La crise du socialisme mondial.* Compare Wauters: *L'évolution du marxisme*, Brussels, 1924.

[20] *La réforme du réformisme?* Brussels, 1926.

[21] See also Vandervelde: *Faut-il changer notre programme?* Brussels, 1923; Hyndman: *The Economics of Socialism*, 1922; S. and B. Webb: *A Constitution for the Socialist Commonwealth of Great Britain*, London, 1920.

[22] See Charles Rappoport: *Jean Jaurès*, 3rd edition, 1925, who quotes much from Jaurès, and Henri Sée: *Jean Jaurès et la doctrine de l'évolution révolutionnaire*, in the *Grande Revue*, November, 1924.

[23] Op. cit., Conclusion.

[24] As early as 1850 Engels considered the Ten Hour Law to be essential for workingmen (*Die Englische Zehnstundenbill*, in *Aus dem literarischen Nachlass*, vol. III, pp. 384–395).

[25] See the observations of Mehring: Ibid., vol. III, pp. 279 ff.

[26] A remark quoted by Bernstein, op. cit., p. 212. In *Le marxisme et son critique Bernstein* he states (p. 295): "If the great disadvantages of the capitalist mode of production are inherent in its beginnings only and are to diminish afterwards, if the number of property holders increases, if social contrasts become less and less marked, and if the proletariat has more and more chance of becoming independent, or at least

of obtaining a satisfactory situation, what is the good of socialism? If I regarded capitalism as Bernstein does, I frankly confess that I should consider socialism to be a grievous error."

[27] "Verschlechterung der Verhältnisse," says Bernstein in the German original.

[28] *Essays on the Materialistic Conception of History.* Bernstein, on the other hand, considers that to correct what is imperfect in the Marxian doctrine is to serve its cause.

CHAPTER VII

[1] *Considérations sur la marche des idées et des événements dans les temps modernes*, Paris, 1872, pp. 1 ff.

[2] Henri Poincaré considers that chance means simply that "slight causes have produced great effects." *Science and Method*, Ch. IV, p. 410, published by the Science Press as Part III of *The Foundations of Science*, New York, 1913.

[3] Charles Seignobos: *A Political History of Europe Since 1814*, New York, 1899, Conclusion, p. 847.

[4] *Vom geschichtlichen Werden*, Stuttgart, 1925–1926, 2 vols. in 8vo.

[5] See the summary of Lavroff's ideas in the work of Charles Rappoport: *La philosophie de l'histoire comme science de l'évolution*, 2nd edition, Paris, 1925, pp. 259–280.

[6] See Henri Sée: *Science et philosophie de l'histoire*, Part I, Ch. VII, Paris, 1927.

[7] See Paul Viollet: *Le Roi et ses ministres*, Paris, 1912.

[8] See G. Bloch: *La République romaine*, Paris, 1912.

[9] See Henri Sée: *Equisse d'une histoire du régime agraire en Europe aux XVIIIe et XIXe siècles*, Paris, 1921.

[10] French translation, Paris, 1926.

[11] "My starting point," he says, "was the fundamental idea

of historical materialism, namely, that it is not consciousness that determines existence, but existence that determines consciousness."

[12] See also Miller: *Histoire des institutions agraires de la Russie Centrale*, Paris, 1926; J. Kulischer: *Russische Wirtschaftsgeschichte*, Jena, 1925.

[13] See Jacques Lapkès: *La main-d'œuvre agricole en Allemagne de la fin du XVIII siècle jusqu'à l'année 1926*, Paris, 1926, pp. 115 ff. (Thesis for agricultural institute of University of Nancy.)

[14] See Paul Vinagradoff: *Custom and Right*, Oslo, 1925.

[15] *Le droit au produit intégral du travail*, pp. 235 ff.

CHAPTER VIII

[1] Antonio Labriola: *Socialisme et philosophie*, pp. 147 ff. The entire chapter is full of very keen and suggestive observations. In *La ruine du monde antique*, of Georges Sorel, the influence of economic considerations on the Church is set forth in a very confused fashion.

[2] See W. J. Ashley: *An Introduction to English Economic History and Theory*, vol. II, Ch. VI; R. Tawney: *Religion and the Rise of Capitalism*, New York, 1926.

[3] See in this connection the brilliant demonstration of G. Coulton: *The Medieval Village*, 1925, and in particular Appendix 37, pp. 540–543.

[4] See on this subject Max Weber: *Die protestantische Ethik und der Geist des Capitalismus*, 1904–1905, republished in the *Gasemmelte Aufsätze zur Religionssoziologie*, Tübingen, 1920; E. Troeltsch: *Die sozialen Lehren der christlichen Kirchen und Gruppen*, Tübingen, 1912; W. Sombart: *The Jews and Modern Capitalism*, London, 1913; Tawney, op. cit.;

Henri Sée: *Science et philosophie de l'histoire*, Part II, Ch. III.

[5] Antonio Labriola: *Socialisme et philosophie*, p. 162. He admits that the "ideologic contents of Plato's dialogues" cannot be understood at once by merely studying the economic structure of Athens. At the same time, Plato cannot be separated from his environment.

[6] See also H. Pirenne: *Histoire de Belgique*, vol. III; Haldvan Koht: *Le problème des origines de la Renaissance* in the *Revue de synthèse historique*, June, 1924; A. Renaudet: *Les influences orientales dans la "divine Comédie et dans la peinture toscane*, in the same journal, December, 1925.

[7] Compare Henri Sée: *L'activité commerciale de la Hollande à la fin du XVIIe siècle*, in the *Revue d'histoire économique*, 1926.

[8] See on this subject the judicious observations of V. G. Simkhovitch: *Marxism versus socialism.*

CHAPTER IX

[1] Plékhanof, in *La conception matérialiste de l'histoire*, Paris, published by the *Populaire*, 1927, justly observes that already in the nineteenth century French historians such as Guizot, Augustin Thierry and Mignet attached great importance to the conflict of interests among the different classes.

[2] See Paul Guiraud: *Etudes économiques sur l'antiquité*, pp. 13 and 46. Compare J. Delevsky: *Antagonismes sociaux et antagonismes prolétariens*, Paris, 1924, pp. 148 ff.

[3] Charles Andler: *La conception matérialiste de l'histoire* in the *Revue de métaphysique et de morale*, 1897, pp. 652 ff.

[4] Fustel de Coulanges: *Le colonat romain (Recherches sur quelques problèms d'histoire*, Paris, 1885); Henri Sée: *Les*

classes rurales et le régime domanial en France au moyen âge, Paris, 1901.

[5] See Henri Sée: *Modern Capitalism: Its Origins and Evolution*, Adelphi Company, 1928.

[6] *Capital*, vol. III, Ch. XXX, p. 561.

[7] Compare pp. 460 and 468 of the same work: "In the interest-bearing capital, therefore, this automatic fetish is elaborated in its pure state, it is self-expanding value, money generating money, and in this form it does not carry any more scars of its origin. The social relation is perfected into the relation of a thing, of money, to itself. Instead of the actual transformation of money into capital, only an empty form meets us here. . . . Now, in the interest-bearing capital the idea of a capitalistic fetish is perfected, the idea, which attributes to the accumulated product of labor, and at that in the fixed form of money, the power of creating surplus-value by its inherent secret qualities, in a purely automatic manner, and in geometrical progression, so that the accumulated product of labor, as the *Economist* thinks, has long discounted all the wealth of the world for all times as belonging to it and coming to it by right." He further shows credit (Ibid. p. 522) as developing "the incentive of capitalistic production, the accumulation of wealth by the appropriation and exploitation of the labor of others, to the purest and most colossal form of gambling and swindling, and reduces more and more the number of those who exploit the social wealth."

[8] In a more subtle form H. Truchy, in his *Cours d'économie politique*, Paris, 1921, vol. II, p. 240, sums up this argument: ". . . Economic society must not be represented as two antithetic personages, the wage earner and the capitalist, one gaining what the other loses. The division of the social product between labor and capital does not in the least give a complete idea of the division of property between individuals. Individual

incomes may at the same time include income from labor and income from capital."

[9] Marx believed that the triumph of the proletariat would abolish all social classes. See *The Poverty of Philosophy*, p. 159.

[10] *Le mouvement ouvrier au début de la monarchie de juillet (1830–1848)*, Paris, 1901. Compare Henri Sée: *La vie économique de la France sous la monarchie censitaire*, Paris, 1927.

[11] See E. Halevy: *Histoire du peuple anglais au XIX siècle*, vol. III, p. 306.

[12] According to Henri de Man, *Au-delà du marxisme*, pp. 28 ff., it was at first purely emotional, and is in many cases not so old as the struggles.

[13] *Vom geschichtlichen Werden*, vol. I, Berlin, 1925.

[14] G. Bloch, op. cit., pp. 23 ff.

[15] Kautsky, in *Die Klassengegensätze im Zeitalter der französischen Revolution*, shows that in the two groups of privileged and non-privileged several classes could be distinguished with divergent interests, and that the sans-culottes themselves included members of the lower middle class, artisans and proletarians.

[16] P. 41.

[17] *Antagonismes sociaux et antagonismes prolétariens*.

[18] Note in this connection that Karl Marx, in his *Revolution and Counter-Revolution or Germany in 1848*, pp. 58 ff., attaches too little importance to the national sentiments of the Slav populations, which, he says, would not be manifested without the support of Russia. As to Bohemia, it can "only exist henceforth as a portion of Germany. . . ."

[19] Delevsky also refers pointedly to the attitude of the workingmen of the various countries during the war, and notably that of the German workers, who did not hesitate to make common cause with their compatriots. We must note how difficult

it would have been in this case for the working class to attempt international action. It would have been necessary to have a much more powerful organization, which, if it had existed, would have removed even the menace of war. On national antagonisms in the working class see Henri de Man, op. cit., pp. 257 ff.

CHAPTER X

[1] See Henri Pirenne: *Histoire de Belgique*, vol. VI, Brussels, 1926, pp. 340 ff.

[2] *La révolution de février*, Paris, 1912 (thesis for the degree of doctor of letters.

[3] Op. cit. pp. 41, 42. Italics ours.

[4] See in this connection Henri Sée: *Esquisse d'une histoire du Régime agraire aux XVIIIe et XIXe siècles*, Paris, 1921. The economic situation of France under the Restoration very closely resembled that of the old regime. See also Henri Sée: *La vie économique de la France sous la monarchie censitaire*, 1927.

[5] See Henry Hamilton: *The English Brass and Copper Industries to 1800*, London, 1926; Ashton: *The Iron and Steel Industry in the Industrial Revolution*, 1924. Paul Barth, op. cit., pp. 58 ff., observes that even class conflicts usually end in compromise, as witness the struggle between patricians and plebs in Rome, the French Revolution, etc.

[6] See Ernst Troeltsch: *Der Historismus und seine Probleme*. Also the recent discussion at the *Centre de synthèse historique*, in the *Revue de synthèse historique*, June, 1926; Henri Sée: *Science et philosophie de l'histoire*, Part II, Ch. I; von Below: *Ueber historische Periodisierungen*, Berlin, 1925.

NOTES

CHAPTER XI

[1] See in this connection the judicious observations of E. R. A. Seligman, op. cit., pp. 109–10, and of V. G. Simkhovitch, op. cit., pp. 40 ff.

[2] *The Economic Interpretation of History*, New York, 1888, p. 12.

[3] Cunningham, on the contrary, in *The Growth of English Industry and Commerce*, deals with economic phenomena as directly determined by political circumstances.

[4] W. Ashley: Surveys Historic and Economic, London, 1900, pp. 22 ff.

[5] *Ueber Entwicklungsgeschichte* in the *Deutsche Zeitschrift für Geschichtswissenschaft*, September, 1896.

[6] *Die Aufgabe der Kulturgeschichte*, 1889. In regard to the above remarks compare Henri Pirenne: *Une polémique historique en Allemagne*, in the *Revue historique*, 1897, vol. LXIV, pp. 50 ff.

[7] A striking sign of the interest in the subject is the number of journals devoted to economic history today. *The Economic History Review* was founded in England in 1927, the *Journal of Business and Economic History* in the United States in 1928, and the *Annales d'histoire économique et sociale* in France in 1929.

[8] Clark: *The Anglo-Dutch Alliance and the War against French Trade*, 1923; S. Elzinga: *Het voorspel van den oorlog van 1672*, Haarlem, 1926.

[9] *L'Inde et le monde*, Paris, 1926.

[10] See Henri Hauser: *De l'humanisme et de la Réforme en France*, in *Etudes sur la Réforme française*, Paris, 1909.

[11] See Aug. Renaudet: *Erasme, sa pensée religieuse et son*

145

action, d'après sa correspondance, Paris, 1926 (*Bibl. de la Revue historique*). If Erasmus failed in his attempt to reconcile Luther's reformation and the church, it was because he encountered opposing political powers and material forces.

[12] On this subject see Cournot: *Considérations sur la marche des idées et des événements dans les temps modernes,* Paris, 1872 ; Henri Sée: *Remarques sur la philosophie de l'histoire de Cournot* in the *Revue de synthèse historique,* December, 1926.

[13] See Henri Sée: *Science et philosophie, de l'histoire,* Part I, Ch. VII.

[14] E. Bernstein: Op. cit., pp. 6 ff.

[15] In the opinion of Seignobos, the phenomena of economic life are completely dominated by political phenomena. See the preface to the seventh edition of his *Histoire politique de l'Europe contemporaine,* 1924, p. xii: "The crisis from which we have been suffering for ten years, and which is assuredly of political origin, makes us feel that such accidents decide the fate of nations; it forces us to recognize *to what extent the superficial phenomena of political life dominate the deep-lying phenomena of economic, intellectual and social life.*" This is equivalent to saying that accident and chance play a predominant part, for "a slight accident is sufficient to upset" the unstable equilibrium of political phenomena.

[16] In our day not only uncompromising marxists like Bukharin (See *L'économie mondiale et l'impérialisme, Paris,* 1928), but also better qualified historians are inclined to see only the economic causes of war. These are undeniable but they are not the only ones: the Italian war of 1859, the campaign of Sadowa in 1866, the Franco-German war of 1870 were provoked especially by the partially idealistic principle of nationality, which also played a certain part in the outbreak of the World War.

NOTES

CHAPTER XII

[1] See Charles Andler: *Introduction au Manifeste communiste.*

[2] *Essays on the Materialistic Conception of History*, p. 244.

[3] P. 119.

[4] Vol. I, Ch. XV, p. 526.

[5] *La conception matérialiste de l'histoire*, pp. 627–658.

[6] On this subject see E. Meyerson: *De l'explication dans les sciences*, 1921, and *La déduction relativiste*, 1925.

[7] See Henri Sée: *Science et philosophie de l'histoire.*

[8] See the most conscientious of them, Auguste Cochin: *Les sociétés de pensée et la démocratie*, 1921; *Les sociétés de pensée et les origines de la Révolution en Bretagne*, Paris, 1925. See also Gaston Martin: *La franc-maçonnerie et la préparation de la Révolution*, Paris, 1926.

[9] See Henri Sée: *Science et philosophie de l'histoire*, Part II, Ch. IV.

[10] See Henri Sée: *L'évolution de la pensée politique en France au XVIIIe siècle*, Paris, 1925.

[11] See also on this subject Henri Sée: *Science and philosophie de l'histoire*, Part II, Ch. III.

[12] It must be remembered that they borrowed many elements from other theorists.

[13] In this connection see the judicious reflections of M. M. Bober: *Karl Marx's Interpretation of History*, Cambridge, Mass. 1927.

BIBLIOGRAPHY

Andler, Charles. *Introduction au manifeste communiste,* Paris, 1901. 11th Edition, 1925;—*La conception matérialiste de l'histoire (Revue de métaphysique et de morale,* 1895, pp. 652 ff.).

Ashley, W. J. *Surveys Historic and Economic,* London, 1900.

Barbagallo, C. *Che cosa è il materialismo storico,* Milan, 1925 *(Nuova rivista storica,* vols. VIII and IX).

Barth, Paul. *Die Geschichtsphilosophie Hegel's und der Hegelianer bis auf Marx und Hartmann,* Leipzig, 1900.

Basch, Victor. *Les doctrines politiques des philosophes classiques de l'Allemagne,* Paris, 1927.

Bernstein, Eduard. *Evolutionary Socialism: A Criticism and an Affirmation,* translated by E. C. Harvey, New York, 1909.

Bloch, G. *La République romaine,* Paris, 1912.

Bober, M. M. *Karl Marx's Interpretation of History,* Harvard Economic Studies, 1927.

Bourguin, Maurice. *Les systèmes socialistes et l'évolution économique,* Paris, 1904.

Breysig, Kurt. *Vom geschichtlichen Werden,* vols. I and II, 1925–26.

Bukharin, N. *Historical Materialism,* New York, 1925.

Cornelissen. *La dialectique dans l'œuvre de Karl Marx (Socialistische Monatshefte,* 1898; translated in the *Revue Socialiste,* February, 1901).

Cournot, A. *Considérations sur la marche des idées et des événements dans les temps modernes,* Paris, 1872.

Croce, Benedetto. *Historical Materialism and the Economics of Karl Marx*, New York, 1914.

Delevsky, J. *Antagonismes sociaux et antagonismes prolétariens*, Paris, 1924.

de Man, Henri. *Au-delà du marxisme*, Brussels, 1927.

Engels, F. *The Condition of the Working Class in England in 1844*, translated by F. K. Wischnewetzky, London, 1892; —*Landmarks of Scientific Socialism (Anti-Dühring)*, translated and edited by Austin Lewis, Chicago, 1907. In German: *Herrn Eugen Dühring's Umwälzung der Wissenschaft*, 10th edition, Stuttgart, 1919.

Festy, O. *Le mouvement ouvrier au début de la monarchie de juillet*, Paris, 1901.

Jaurès, Jean. *De primis socialismi germani lineamentis apud Lutherum, Kant, Fichte et Hegel*, Paris, 1891 (thesis for doctor of letters. French translation in the *Revue Socialiste*, June-August, 1892).

Jaurès, Jean. *Etudes socialistes*, Paris, 1902;—*Bernstein et l'évolution de la Méthode socialiste*, 1910, Paris, 1926 (pamphlet).

Kautsky, K. *Die Klassengegensätze im Zeitalter der französischen Revolution*, 1889, 2nd edition, Stuttgart, 1908;— *Die materialistische Geschichtsauffassung*, Berlin, 1927, 2 vols. in 8vo;—*Le marxisme et son critique Bernstein*, translated by Martin-Leray, Paris, 1901.

Labriola, Antonio. *Essays on the Materialistic Conception of History*, translated by Charles H. Kerr, Chicago, 1904;— *Socialisme et philosophie*, Paris, 1899.

Labriola, Arturo. *Il capitalismo*, Naples, 1926.

Langlois, Ch. V. and Seignobos, Ch. *Introduction to the Study of History*, translated by G. G. Berry, New York, 1912.

Lescure, Jean. *Des crises générales et périodiques de surproduction*, Bordeaux, 1906, 3rd edition, Paris, 1926.

BIBLIOGRAPHY

Loria, Achille. *Les bases économiques de la constitution sociale*, Paris, 1893;—*Les fondements rationnels du matérialisme économique* (*Annales de l'Institut international de sociologie*, vol. VIII, 1902;—*La Constituzione economica odierna*, Turin, 1900;—*The Economic Synthesis*, translated by M. Eden Paul, London, 1914.

Marx, Karl. *Capital, A Critique of Political Economy*, Vol. I. *The Process of Capitalist Production*, translated by Samuel Moore and Edward Aveling, Chicago, 1921; Vol. II. *The Process of Circulation of Capital*, translated by Ernest Untermann, Chicago, 1919; Vol. III. *The Process of Capitalistic Production as a Whole*, translated by Ernest Untermann, Chicago, 1909;—*Critique de l'économie politique*, translated by Remy, Paris, 1899. In English: *The Critique of Political Economy*, Chicago, 1907;—*The Communist Manifesto*, Chicago, 1915. In French: *Le Manifeste communiste*, Paris, 1901; —*Le 18 brumaire de Louis Bonaparte*. In English: *The Eighteenth Brumaire of Louis Bonaparte*, translated by Daniel de Leon, Chicago, 1914;—*Le lutte des classes en France de 1848 à 1850*. In German: *Die Klassenkämpfe in Frankreich, 1848 bis 1850*, Berlin, 1911;—*The Poverty of Philosophy*, translated by H. Quelch, London, 1900;—*Revolution and Counter-Revolution or Germany in 1848*, edited by Eleanor Marx Aveling, New York, 1896.*

* A new set of *Oeuvres complètes* of Karl Marx is now being published by A. Costes, Paris, translated by J. Molitor.)

Mehring, Franz. *Aus dem literarischen Nachlass von Karl Marx, Fr. Engels, und F. Lassalle*, 3 vols. Stuttgart, 1902.

Menger, A. *Le droit au produit intégral du travail*, French translation, Paris, 1900.

Meyerson, Emile. *De l'explication dans les sciences*, Paris, 1921, 2 vols. in 8vo.

Mondolfo, Rodolfo. *Le matérialisme historique d'après Frédéric Engels*, French translation, Paris, 1917.

Pareto, Vilfredo. *Les systèmes socialistes*, Paris, 1902.

Philip, André. *Henri de Man et la crise doctrinale du socialisme*, Paris, 1928.

Pirenne, Henri. *Histoire de Belgique*, 6 vols. in 8vo;—*Les étapes de l'histoire sociale du capitalisme* (*Bulletin de l'Académie de Belgique*, 1914). [Translation: "The Stages in the Social History of Capitalism," Am. Hist. Review, Apr., 1914, pp. 454 f.] ; *Medieval Cities*, Princeton Press, 1924.

Plékhanof, Georges. *La conception matérialiste de l'histoire*, published by the *Populaire*, Paris, 1917;—*Introduction à l'histoire sociale de la Russie*, Paris, 1926 (Institut des Etudes slaves) ;—*Les questions fondamentales du Marxisme*, Paris, 1927.

Rappoport, Ch. *La philosophie de l'histoire comme science de l'évolution*, 2nd edition, Paris, 1926;—*Jean Jaurès*, 3rd edition, Paris, 1925.

Riazanov, D. *Karl Marx and Friedrich Engels*, translated by J. Kunitz, New York, 1927.

Rogers, James E. Thorold. *The Economic Interpretation of History*, New York, 1889.

Sée, Henri. *Esquisse d'une histoire du régime agraire en Europe aux XVIIIe et XIXe siècles*, Paris, 1921;—*L'évolution commerciale et industrielle de la France sous l'ancien régime*, Paris, 1925;—*Economic and Social Conditions in France during the 18th Century*, translated by E. H. Zeydel, New York, 1927;—*Modern Capitalism: Its Origins and Evolution* translated by H. B. Vanderblue and Georges Doriot, New York, 1928; *Science et philosophie de l'histoire*, Paris, 1928.

Seignobos, Ch. *Histoire politique de l'Europe contemporaine*,

BIBLIOGRAPHY

7th edition, Paris, 1916. In English: *A Political History of Europe Since 1814*, New York, 1899— An early edition, number not specified.

Seligman, E. R. A. *The Economic Interpretation of History*, New York, 1902.

Simkhovitch, V. G. *Marxism versus Socialism*, New York, 1913.

Sombart, Werner. *Der moderne Kapitalismus*, 4th edition, 1922, 2 "vols"—(each separated into "halves"—The Dritter Band, also in two "halves" did not appear until 1927–28; Subtitle: *Das Wirtschaftsleben im Zeitalter des Hochkapitalismus*);—*The Jews and Modern Capitalism*, London, 1913;—*Friedrich Engels*, Berlin, 1895.

Sorel, Georges. *La ruine du monde antique: conception matérialiste de l'histoire*, 2nd edition, Paris, 1925.

Tawney, R. H. *Religion and the Rise of Capitalism*, London, 1926.

Tönnies, F. *Neuere Philosophie der Geschichte: Hegel, Marx, Comte* (Archiv für Geschichte der Philosophie, vol. VII, 1894).

Troeltsch, E. *Der Historismus und seine Probleme*, Tübingen, 1922.

Turgeon, Ch. *La conception matérialiste de l'histoire d'après Ant. Labriola et Ach. Loria* (Travaux juridiques et économiques de l'Université de Rennes, vol. III, 1911).

Vinogradoff, P. *Custom and Right*, Oslo and Paris, 1925.

Vandervelde, Emile. *La psychologie du socialisme à propos de trois livres récents*, *Mémoires de l'Académie de Belgique*, Tome 22, fasc. 3, 1928;—*Le Marxisme a-t'il fait faillite*, Brussels, 1928.

Wauters, O. *L'évolution du marxisme*, Brussels, 1924.

Weber, Max. *Gesammelte Aufsätze zur Religionssoziologie*,

ECONOMIC INTERPRETATION OF HISTORY
Tübingen, 1920;—*General Economic History*, translated by F. H. Knight, New York, 1927.

Woltmann, Ludwig. *Der historische Materialismus*, Düsseldorf, 1900.